More Praise for *When Money Talks*

"When money talks, democracy walks. Read this book to learn how We the People can take back our elections from the billionaires and overturn a Supreme Court ruling that is a gross misreading of our Constitution."

—Robert B. Reich, Chancellor's Professor, University of California, Berkeley, and former US Secretary of Labor

"Derek Cressman nails it: money isn't speech; it's power. After the Supreme Court's folly in *Citizens United*, concentrated money and power is destroying our democracy. But we can save it with a twenty-eighth amendment to the Constitution, and this book shows all of us how. Read it and join this historic work of all Americans."

—Jeff Clements, author of *Corporations Are Not People*

"Derek Cressman has explored the great issues of money in politics from every perspective: as a scholarly observer, as a passionate activist, as a serious candidate. And he has drawn from his years of struggle on behalf of nothing less than democracy itself an essential insight: 'If money is speech, then speech is no longer free.' Cressman's brilliant examination of all the questions, all the ideas, all the issues that extend from that statement provides an essential starting point for every discussion of how to fix our broken electoral and governing systems. *When Money Talks* is much more than a book—although it is a very fine book. It is the key we have been looking for to unlock a future where the will of the people again triumphs over the money power."

—John Nichols, Washington correspondent, *The Nation*

"The movement to overturn *Citizens United* is turning into a stampede. Derek Cressman is helping lead the way. Read *When Money Talks* and join the movement."

—Ben Cohen, cofounder, Ben & Jerry's Ice Cream, and Head Stamper, StampStampede.org

"Cressman's book is a powerful indictment of *Citizens United* and provides thoughtful ideas on how We the People can help restore our democracy."

—Lisa Graves, Executive Director, Center for Media and Democracy, and publisher, PRWatch.org and ALECexposed.org

"Already, sixteen states and some 650 localities have called on Congress to send the states a constitutional amendment overturning *Citizens United*. In two states, Colorado and Montana, voters sent the message directly, through ballot measures that Derek Cressman helped lead when he was a vice president at Common Cause. We can thank Derek for his early, strategic thinking and organizing that built momentum for a constitutional amendment as the people's solution to the problem."

—From the epilogue by Miles Rapoport, President, Common Cause

"When the story is written about how Americans came together to overturn *Citizens United* and end billionaire rule, Derek Cressman will have his own chapter. His passion for democracy is exceeded only by his clarity and his insights. *When Money Talks* is a map to the twenty-eighth amendment goal line."

—Michele Sutter, cofounder, Money Out Voters In Coalition

"For more than twenty years, Derek Cressman has been at the vanguard calling for a constitutional amendment to end the big-money dominance of our elections. *When Money Talks* powerfully makes the case why our current system of unlimited campaign spending is a threat to our republic and how we can advance and win a twenty-eighth amendment to ensure that all voices can be heard in the political process on a level playing field. Derek Cressman is a visionary for our democracy, and this is a must-read book for all Americans, across the political spectrum, who want to take the country back from the oligarchs and reclaim it for We the People."

—John Bonifaz, cofounder and President, Free Speech for People

"There aren't many people who can cut through the legalese and fine print surrounding the complicated issue of money in politics as cogently as Derek Cressman. This book shows yet again that he is one of the most thoughtful, effective leaders in the fight to take back our democracy."

—Michael B. Keegan, President, People for the American Way

When
Money
Talks

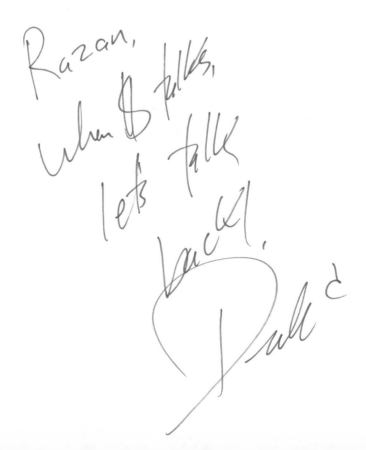

Razan,

When $ talks,
let's talk

back!.

Dan d

When Money Talks

The High Price of "Free" Speech and the Selling of Democracy

Derek D. Cressman

BK

Berrett–Koehler Publishers, Inc.
a BK Currents book

Berrett-Koehler Publishers, Inc.
1333 Broadway, Suite 1000
Oakland, CA 94612-1921
Tel: (510) 817-2277   Fax: (510) 817-2278   www.bkconnection.com

Ordering Information

Quantity sales. Special discounts are available on quantity purchases by corporations, associations, and others. For details, contact the "Special Sales Department" at the Berrett-Koehler address above.

Individual sales. Berrett-Koehler publications are available through most bookstores. They can also be ordered directly from Berrett-Koehler:
Tel: (800) 929-2929; Fax: (802) 864-7626; www.bkconnection.com

Orders for college textbook/course adoption use. Please contact Berrett-Koehler:
Tel: (800) 929-2929; Fax: (802) 864-7626.

Orders by U.S. trade bookstores and wholesalers. Please contact Ingram Publisher Services, Tel: (800) 509-4887; Fax: (800) 838-1149; E-mail: customer.service@ingrampublisherservices.com; or visit www.ingrampublisher services.com/Ordering for details about electronic ordering.

Berrett-Koehler and the BK logo are registered trademarks of Berrett-Koehler Publishers, Inc.

Printed in the United States of America

Berrett-Koehler books are printed on long-lasting acid-free paper. When it is available, we choose paper that has been manufactured by environmentally responsible processes. These may include using trees grown in sustainable forests, incorporating recycled paper, minimizing chlorine in bleaching, or recycling the energy produced at the paper mill.

Library of Congress Cataloging-in-Publication Data

Names: Cressman, Derek D., author.
Title: When money talks : the high price of "free" speech and the selling of democracy / Derek D. Cressman.
Description: First edition. | Oakland, CA : Berrett-Koehler Publishers, Inc., [2016] | Includes bibliographical references and index.
Identifiers: LCCN 2015024932 | ISBN 9781626565760 (pbk. : acid-free paper)
Subjects: LCSH: Campaign funds—Law and legislation—United States. | Freedom of speech—United States.
Classification: LCC KF4920 .C74 2016 | DDC 323.44/30973—dc23
LC record available at http://lccn.loc.gov/2015024932

First Edition

21 20 19 18 17 16   10 9 8 7 6 5 4 3 2 1

Interior design and project management: Dovetail Publishing Services
Cover design: Irene Morris Design

For Senator Fritz Hollings,
who fought the good fight
when no one else would.

Contents

Foreword

by Thom Hartmann

In this book, Derek Cressman makes the powerful and persuasive claim that by "enhancing" freedom of speech through its *Citizens United* ruling (and others), the US Supreme Court has done real damage to actual freedom of political speech in America. So much damage, in fact, that our democratic republic is now in a serious crisis and heading in a very, very bad direction.

Cressman, with elegant examples, shows how historically we have actually *enhanced* political free speech by *regulating* it, be it time limits for public input at a city council meeting or the time limits for debate in Congress.

And he shows how, by embracing a radical, libertarian-like position of laissez-faire with regard to money in politics, the Supreme Court has driven our democratic process of electing representatives totally off the rails. (Keep in mind that the entire "libertarian" concept, and then the Libertarian Party itself, were devised and created in the 1940s by the nation's largest business groups to provide a moral/intellectual/legal argument for diminishing the ability of government to "meddle" in the business of this country's largest corporations.)

Spending money was historically considered a "behavior" and thus could be regulated (as we particularly did in the early 1970s after the Nixon corruption scandals). With the

Buckley v. Valeo decision in 1976, the Supreme Court flipped more than two hundred years of legal precedent on its head by ruling that investing money in politicians and the political process was protected by the "free speech" provision of the First Amendment. The result—now on steroids with the 2010 *Citizens United* expansion of that SCOTUS doctrine—has been pretty easy to see.

In a democracy, you'd assume that the desires of the majority of the people would determine the content and probability of passage of legislation, from the local to the federal level. And, indeed, for much of America's history that's how it worked, particularly in the middle of the twentieth century. (*Who* was enfranchised to vote also swung things, but that's another argument for another book.) But those days are gone. Elected officials now disregard the desires of the people and focus instead on pleasing the billionaires.

Unregulated political "free speech" is a virtual oxymoron, like a "free football game" would be. In sports, we're quite used to rules and regulations: they make the game fair for everybody involved. But if the logic the Supreme Court has applied to the spending of money for political persuasion were applied to football, the game would be quite different. Whichever team had the most money could pay to rewrite the rules to determine where to put their goalposts, for example, or where to kick off and kick field goals from. A rich team, putting the goalposts on its own ten-yard line, would only have a ninety-yard field to worry about; the poorer team would have to play the full hundred yards.

Imagine if the referees in a football game were supplied by the teams, fifty-fifty, but it took a majority of them to conclude a call on a play. And then one of the teams told their referees never to agree to call any penalties against "their" team. How could anybody call that a "fair game"?

It's reminiscent of the 2015 announcement by Federal Election Commission chair Ann M. Ravel that the three Republicans on the six-person board of the FEC refused to allow the FEC to consider any consequential enforcement of federal election laws (it takes four votes to proceed with an action against a donor or candidate). Billionaires and corporations heavily favor the Republicans in their political spending, and the Republican appointees on the FEC board want to keep it that way. As the Associated Press and the *New York Times* reported on May 2, 2015: "She [Chairwoman Ravel] says she has now essentially abandoned efforts to work out agreements on what she sees as much-needed enforcement measures."[1]

Just like in sports, business, or society in general, politics only works honestly if it operates within well-understood, transparent rules that everybody agrees to follow. When the unelected Supreme Court—not a legislature, not a president or governor, not a single elected official in the history of our nation—said that the rules pertaining to the spending of money passed by Congress and signed by several presidents shouldn't be enforced, political anarchy was the predictable result (as explained in detail in John Paul Stevens' dissent in *Citizens United*).

The result is that the first viability test for political candidates for our highest offices is a simple question: "How many billionaires and transnational corporations support you?" And that's not democracy; it's the antithesis of the republic our Founders envisaged.

As I've noted in previous books and articles, even our Founders thought the idea that turning a nation's political and economic systems over to "free market" corporatists is idiotic. Moreover, they warned us of an overreaching judiciary turning into an oligarchy, as Thomas Jefferson wrote to William Charles Jarvis in 1820:

> *You seem to consider the federal judges as the ultimate arbiters of all constitutional questions, a very dangerous doctrine, indeed, and one which would place us under the despotism of an oligarchy. Our judges are as honest as other men, and not more so. They have with others the same passions for the party, for power and the privilege of the corps. Their power is the more dangerous, as they are in office for life and not responsible, as the other functionaries are, to the elective control. The Constitution has erected no such single tribunal, knowing that to whatever hands confided, with the corruptions of time and party, its members would become despots. It has more wisely made all departments co-equal and co-sovereign within themselves.*[2]

In a letter to Samuel Kercheval, Jefferson put his faith in the people, not the courts or the wealthy: "I am not among those who fear the people. They, and not the rich, are our dependence for continued freedom. . . . We must make our election between *economy* and *liberty*, or *profusion* and *servitude*. . . . [Otherwise], as the people of England are, our people, like them, must come to labor sixteen hours in the twenty-four . . . and the sixteenth being insufficient to afford us bread, we must live, as they now do, on oatmeal and potatoes; have no time to think, no means of calling the mismanagers to account; but be glad to obtain subsistence by hiring ourselves to rivet their chains on the necks of our fellow-sufferers."[3]

A totally "free" market where corporations reign supreme, just like the oppressive governments of old, Jefferson said, could transform America "till the bulk of the society is reduced to be mere automatons of misery, and to have no sensibilities left but for sinning and suffering. Then begins, indeed, the *bellum omnium in omnia* [war of all against all], which some philosophers observing to be so general in this world, have mistaken it for the natural, instead of the abusive state of man."

Derek Cressman, virtually channeling Jefferson, has elegantly assembled a startling and motivating summary of how far our political process has degenerated as a result of these Supreme Court rulings, and offers some very specific solutions. Read on!

Introduction

The Crisis of Broken Politics

We know now that government by organized money is just as dangerous as government by organized mob.
—Franklin D. Roosevelt

Gayle McGlaughlin had no choice. When Reverend Kenneth Davis ignored her fifth warning that he had exceeded his time for speaking at the city council meeting and was out of order, the mayor of Richmond, California, had police remove Reverend Davis from the council chambers.

The mayor limited Reverend Davis's speech, and rightly so. Twenty-six people waited to speak during the opening public comment period. Each was given one minute.

Many of the speakers, including Kenneth Davis, stayed beyond public comment to share more opinions. Reverend Davis wanted to talk about a council member he had once endorsed who had subsequently been rude to him and told him to "shut up." He wanted to criticize an elected official, or as our Constitution says, "petition the Government for a redress of grievances."

1

The meeting dragged on until nearly midnight that night of February 12, 2012, even with the mayor enforcing the time limits. Vice Mayor Jim Rogers pointed out that lengthy public comments meant the council routinely addressed important issues after 11:00 p.m. Many people could not stay that long and lost their chance to speak.

The First Amendment to the United States Constitution tells us government may not make laws "abridging the freedom of speech" of "the people." Yet the First Amendment did not die that day in Richmond when the government limited one person's speech. That's because those limits gave other people a chance to speak—an equal chance. The *people's* freedom of speech is enhanced by limiting how long each *person* speaks.

Beyond good manners, it's just plain common sense to sit down, be quiet, and listen to others after you've said your piece. Walk into a room of first graders who are all talking at once and you realize that nobody can be heard unless everyone takes turns. Sometimes the teacher must ignore the hands of students who have spoken frequently and call on the quieter members of the class. As voters, we'll make better decisions about public matters when we hear from everyone, not just a noisy few. Two heads are better than one, so the saying goes, but only if you hear from both of them.

Similarly, because we expand speech overall by limiting each speaker, Congress limits the time a representative can talk on the floor of Congress. We strictly limit each candidate's speech during presidential debates. Even the Supreme Court strictly limits the number of pages in legal briefs as well as the amount of time lawyers have to present their case during oral arguments. It's only fair to make sure all sides of an issue get equal time, and it's more likely that Congress and the Court will make a wise decision after hearing a balanced debate.

But when it comes to money in political campaigns, the Supreme Court of the United States has turned this commonsense principle of fairness and sound decision-making on its head. Five zealots on the Court say the First Amendment forbids limiting the amount of money a billionaire like Charles Koch or Tom Steyer spends to promote his point of view. These five men in black robes say it is unconstitutional to prevent the super-rich from drowning out the voices of everyone else.

These five men are wrong.

And the rest of us must make it right.

It has become fashionable to say that American politics is "broken." Voter participation rates are plummeting, partisan bickering gridlocks Washington, and government fails to solve our biggest problems. There are dozens of "money in politics" books and reports that "connect the dots" between campaign contributions and policy outcomes. If you are unfamiliar with the ways big money unduly influences public policy, then those books are for you.

This book is for those who already know that American politics is broken and who want to repair it. If you have moved beyond cynicism to action but are unsure how to prevail when the deck is stacked against us, then this book is for you. We'll explore strategies such as voter instruction ballot measures that previous generations of Americans have used to overcome similar problems. We'll examine how we can raise our collective voice and force a stubborn, self-interested Congress to change the way it gets elected.

"If you have moved beyond cynicism to action but are
unsure how to prevail when the deck is stacked against us,
then this book is for you."

Who Broke Our Democracy and How Did They Get Away with It?

Our political system didn't just break. Somebody broke it.
That means we can repair it. Public dialogue has not always
been overwhelmed with big money, and it need not be in the
future. Understanding how and why specific people broke
our government is our first step toward mending it.

This book will describe infamous Supreme Court rulings such as *Citizens United v. Federal Election Commission*,
Buckley v. Valeo, and other cases that have broken our
democracy. We'll examine how judges who have never run
for any office have struck down numerous campaign finance
laws passed with bipartisan support over a period of forty
years. These include laws enacted directly by the people
themselves through ballot initiatives and passed by overwhelming majorities. We are confronting one of the most
brazen periods of sustained judicial overreach in our nation's
history.[4] Over the past four decades, our least accountable
branch of government has shackled the other two branches
and the steadfast will of the People.

The extreme imbalance of speech in our political campaigns produces a Congress and a public conversation that
do not accurately represent the political viewpoints of the
American people. Members of Congress are generally older,
richer, and whiter than we are as a people. They listen far
more to the wealthiest in our society than they do to the

middle class (forgetting the poor altogether), because the wealthy determine who gets elected to Congress.

We are no longer conducting elections but rather holding auctions. The candidate for Congress who spends the most in the campaign wins nine out of ten times.[5] Although this is philosophically troubling, it would be tolerable if we could all bid in the auction. But we can't.

Only about 4 percent of Americans make a political contribution during any given election cycle, a figure that is declining over time.[6] Most donors give $25, maybe $50 dollars to a couple of candidates they really like. Fewer than one in five hundred Americans give more than $200 to any federal candidate.[7]

But the size of the donations given directly to members of Congress and presidential campaigns pale in comparison to the huge checks written to the so-called super PACs (political action committees). More than 3.7 million people gave Mitt Romney and Barack Obama $200 or less in the 2012 election—amounting to $313 million dollars. They were offset by only thirty-two fat cats—the biggest donors of all—who gave presidential super PACs a comparable amount with an average of $9.9 million each.[8]

Although there are plutocrats supporting both the Democrat and Republican parties, neither side's big donors accurately reflect the views of most Americans. For example, 40 percent of wealthy people believe the minimum wage should be high enough to lift full-time workers out of poverty, whereas 78 percent of the general public believes this.[9]

Money does not buy victory in every election but, in every election, money matters more than it should and in ways we cannot even see. Knowing that the candidate who spends the most money wins almost every time, many citizens who would make excellent legislators don't run because they can't—or won't—do what it takes to raise the money.

When I was considering whether to run for secretary of state in California, I spoke with several bigwigs in my political party who laid out very clearly how much money other candidates would raise and what I'd need to raise to be considered viable to run against them. It was enough to send most sensible people running for the hills, but I decided to give it a try anyway.

I later interviewed with dozens of civic organizations to seek their endorsement, and their most pressing question was how much money had I raised. Sure, they were interested in my policy positions, but they knew the way things work. Organizations that endorsed a candidate who had raised less money than another would likely be on the wrong side of the winner. Not only would that give them less access and influence with the eventual officeholder, but backing a loser would make them look ineffective to their members.

Winning the "wealth primary"[10] by raising the most money allows a candidate to speak more loudly and more frequently than her opponents. It also creates an aura of inevitability about the race, which the news media compounds and magnifies by only covering candidates who have raised big money and further diminishing the opportunity for other candidates to be heard.

Candidates who tackle issues contrary to wealthy interests get moved to the sidelines and those issues vanish from public discourse. Tim Donnelly discovered this the hard way when he ran for governor of California in 2014. A Tea Party conservative, Donnelly ran against fellow Republican Neel

Kashkari. Kashkari was (and still is) a Wall Street hero, having engineered the federal bailout of the banks that crashed our economy in 2008.

The campaign was a battle for the future of the Republican Party in California. Wealthy businessmen worried that Donnelly's conservative views on abortion, guns, and gay marriage would not win over a majority of Californians.

Donnelly outraised Kashkari by a ratio of ten to one among donors who gave less than $100.[11] Although disclosure records do not tell us the total number of donors to either campaign, there is no doubt that significantly more people donated to Donnelly than to Kashkari—it's just that their checks were a lot smaller.

Kashkari raised more than $900,000 from wealthy donors in the first two weeks of his campaign—more than double what Donnelly had raised in the entire year before. Kashkari dumped another $2 million of his own money into his primary campaign—money he'd received in compensation as a Goldman Sachs executive.

Donnelly started at 17 percent in the polls compared to Kashkari's 2 percent.[12] Just weeks before the election, Donnelly still had more support, with 15 percent compared to Kashkari's 10 percent.[13] But, after outspending Donnelly by more than four to one, Kashkari came in at 19.4 percent of the vote to Donnelly's 14.8 percent to win the primary. Neither candidate had a prayer of defeating incumbent governor Jerry Brown in the general election, but big money in the primary meant the November campaign ended up being about Kashkari's attacks on high-speed rail and teacher tenure instead of the issues of tax cuts, gun rights, and social concerns that Donnelly would have raised. In other words, candidates debated issues the wealthy elite cared about, but not the concerns of conservative Californians who had no voice in the general election.

Ask yourself, would our public discourse have been different if both Donnelly and Kashkari spent the same amount of money, instead of one candidate having what amounted to four times the speech of the other? Or, suppose fundraising truly reflected popular support for the candidate and Donnelly had outspent Kashkari by the ten-to-one ratio that Donnelly outraised him among small donors. What then would have happened? We will never know for sure, but we can be certain that big money changed the dynamics of the gubernatorial race in ways that distorted the marketplace of ideas.

More Bad News: A Judicial Coup

As the 2014 California gubernatorial race attests, big money not only influences who wins elections; it allows a tiny and unrepresentative group of people to determine who runs in the first place and what issues we discuss during campaigns.

This is bad news.

It is, in fact, *very* bad news because the capture of our legislative branch by a wealthy elite is compounded by the capture of our judicial branch by the same narrow, wealth-worshipping clan. This judicial coup short-circuits the checks and balances that the Framers of our Constitution put in place to guard against the evils of what they called "faction" (and we call special interests) that they quite correctly predicted would arise in a democratic republic.

Judges are supposed to protect the people from overreaching legislators who deprive us of liberty, whether out of self-interest or due to momentary swings in public passion.

Our Founders feared mob rule, where majorities of voters get caught up in a temporary rage and trample on the rights of minorities. Although large numbers of people are more likely than small numbers of people to accumulate the wisdom of the crowd, even democratic majorities can (and do) make mistakes.

But instead of protecting our republic from temporary mob rule, five of the nine members of our Supreme Court are protecting a powerful but miniscule elite from the People themselves. Instead of mob rule, we have "millionaire rule" by a gang of fat cats who extort our politicians to serve their interests instead of the public at large. Those politicians then choose or approve the judges who sit on the Supreme Court, which works about as well as having the Mafia appoint our police chiefs.

Paid Speech Isn't Free

The same billionaires who have captured our courts have also created a network of think tanks, academics, public relations firms, lawyers, and political consultants to manufacture a plausible reason for us to submit to their rule. They have twisted and perverted the concept of freedom of speech, so cherished by our nation, by claiming it is impossible to limit spending on political campaigns without also censoring the *New York Times*, or jailing comedians who criticize our government through satires like *Saturday Night Live*. I'm not making this up: that's really what Senator Ted Cruz said on the floor of the United States Senate while defending the "rights" of billionaires to buy elections.

The oligarchs try to confuse us by pointing out that spending money can disseminate speech. That's true. But a lot depends on who's paying—a distinction that has been obscured in our campaign finance debate. Exploring this distinction, as we'll do in chapter 2, resolves the so-called "unintended consequences" that opponents of campaign finance reform invent.

Sometimes a speaker pays to get other people to listen to him, as when you purchase a loudspeaker so more people can hear you. Sometimes the listener pays to hear the speech, such as when you buy a ticket to see a political movie.

Usually there is a middleman who is paid by either the speaker or the listener to disseminate speech. Lobbyists are middlemen that are paid by CEOs to promote a corporation's interests to legislators. Book publishers are paid by readers to distribute the speech of authors. The book you are now reading contains political speech, but I'm not paying to make you read it—you paid to buy it, or a library paid to offer it to you.

Perhaps the most important middleman is the news media—the press. Subscribers pay newspapers to provide articles and columns that they actively want to read. Advertisers pay newspapers to include speech that readers don't particularly want to read but will tolerate to subsidize the articles they do want. Consumers pay cable TV providers for programs like Fox News and MSNBC, but advertisers pay even more so they can speak to the captive audience that the programs attract.

When politicians say campaign spending limits violate the First Amendment, their scare tactics rely on a simple trick: they ignore the distinction of who's paying. As the Nobel Prize–winning economist Milton Friedman pointed out, there's no such thing as a free lunch. Likewise, there is no such thing as free speech when someone else is paying for you to hear it.

If you or I are purchasing speech, we are limited only by our wallet and the number of newspapers, magazines, or books available at the local bookstore or, these days, the various sources of information available online. Media consolidation and threats to the Internet's content neutrality could artificially restrict our choices, so we must protect our rights to freely choose the speech we want to hear via these forums.

In a world of Google Books and Project Gutenberg, which is making every book in the public domain available on the Internet for free,[14] we have more opportunities to seek out speech than ever before. A lot of online information may be free once the reader pays an Internet service provider, but that individual is still seeking it out, not having it foisted on her by advertisers. There is no need for legal limits when the listener is buying—to the contrary, the law needs to expand and protect our choices.

But when the speaker is buying speech and pushing it onto a captive audience, we run into real-world limitations on a listener's time. Legislators only have a certain amount of time to listen to constituents. Realistically, they might grant fewer than a dozen meetings a day. When legislators meet with paid lobbyists representing campaign donors, they have less time to hear constituents. Money talks while ordinary citizens are silenced.

Similarly, voters have limited time to consider all the candidates and measures on their ballot. The more time they spend watching ads and reading mailers from big money candidates, the less time they have to consider the messages and positions of other candidates. Low-budget campaigns are drowned out by big money.

I attended the Richmond City Council meeting described at the opening of this chapter to discuss a topic that ultimately wasn't even considered because the rest of the meeting took too long. My speech was, quite literally, pushed off the agenda.[15] Even with the council rules limiting the duration of each speaker, there were so many people who wanted to speak that my voice that night was squelched by the speech of others. Whether it is city councilors listening to public comment, legislators debating on the floors of Congress, or voters considering information about candidates, we all have limited time to listen to various and competing viewpoints. If one person or group pays money to foist its viewpoint on the listener, it crowds out other viewpoints. When we're dealing with a captive audience, we can only expand free speech by limiting paid speech.

Think about it: Should I have been allowed to pay for the privilege of speaking that night? Should others have been able to buy more than a minute's time to talk? Would anyone consider that "free" speech?

To eliminate the confusion being generated by the outright lies of the billionaires and their lackeys in our courts and legislatures, we must draw a clear distinction between paid speech, where the speaker is paying to get others to listen, and free speech, which is equally available to everyone. We need to distinguish the free press, where the listener seeks out information, from paid advertisements, where, in a sense, information seeks out listeners. This is a simple line to draw, but much of our dialogue around campaign finance rules for the past forty years has obscured it. We have instead become mired in complexities of considering which actions are corrupting according to the so-called experts and which ones aren't. Chapter 2 will help sort this out.

Overcoming the Bad News

We face not only *very* bad news, but a complex problem that thwarts the tools of self-government our Founders created to solve problems just like this. We face opponents that are taking advantage of the problem's complexity and trying to buffalo us into believing that it is impossible to have a democracy unless we put our elections up for sale.

The news is not just bad, it's become catastrophic—and, paradoxically, therein lies our salvation.

Nobody wants to hear bad news. Our lives are difficult enough between taking care of sick children, holding down jobs, and taking out the garbage to spend too much time listening to any news at all. But we have almost no time whatsoever for depressing news, especially news we feel we cannot change. There is no point worrying about things we have no control over, so we spend what little free time we have consuming information that's more fun—such as watching a football game or a "reality" TV show. We push bad news out of our minds, shrugging it off as an annoyance we have to live with.

Unlike bad news, catastrophes rouse us to action. We find ways to help, come hell or high water. After Hurricane Katrina hit New Orleans, Americans gave the Red Cross more than $2 billion in relief funds[16]—almost as much to that one organization as the $2.5 billion individuals gave to all federal and state candidates in the year before.[17] The Red Cross mobilized more than seventy-four thousand volunteers in the first two weeks after the storm.

American resolve is also particularly strong in crises that threaten our republic. We sat on the sidelines during the first years of World War II, ignoring the alarming news of

Adolf Hitler's invasion of Europe and his blatant disregard for human rights. But after the Japanese bombing of Pearl Harbor turned the situation into a catastrophe, the United States completely disrupted its economy and the personal lives of every citizen in order to fight external enemies. If we could do that, surely we can defeat our current internal enemies subverting our democracy.

We've solved bigger problems within our republic before, making it more participatory, more just, and wiser. When our nation was founded, only white men who owned property could vote. Expanding the electorate to include non-landowners was against the self-interest of the incumbent politicians and current voters of the time. And yet we did it.

It took a constitutional amendment to include women in our national electorate. Eighteen-year-olds were considered mature enough to go to war but not old enough to vote prior to the passage of the Twenty-sixth Amendment in 1971.

The process to amend the US Constitution is difficult, yet when our resolve is strong, we have made it happen. Seven of our twenty-seven constitutional amendments overturned previous rulings by the Supreme Court. This is how our system of checks and balances works.

Cynics say it would be too difficult to pass a constitutional amendment to overturn the Supreme Court's ruling in *Citizens United*, but the skeptics underestimate Americans and don't appreciate our history. Women in the early twentieth century didn't concede that an amendment was too difficult. They fought to make it happen. Like a sleeping lion finally roused to action by vultures that have stolen her prey one too many times, Americans can make bold, swift changes to take back our rightful heritage of self-government once we fully awaken to the threat.

Naysayers forget that honorable people have risen above their partisan interests when the fate of our republic hung in the balance. It was Republican leaders in Congress, such as Howard Baker, who led the congressional investigation of the Watergate scandal. It was a southern Democrat, Lyndon Johnson, who signed the Civil Rights Act of 1964 while saying "we've just delivered the south to the Republican Party for a long time to come."[18]

By far, the most difficult crisis in our nation's history was slavery, which denied millions of African Americans the inalienable rights of liberty, the pursuit of happiness, and sometimes even life—rights so clearly enshrined for all people in our Declaration of Independence. The economic elite profiting from slavery was larger and more powerful than the billionaires today who have captured our legislatures and courts. Their power was reflected in the Supreme Court, which bolstered the institution of slavery in the *Dred Scott* decision (a powerful reminder that *Citizens United* was not our highest court's first mistake). Yet, government of, by, and for the people beat the slave owners then, and we will beat the billionaires now.

The Worse Things Get, the Bigger We Must Think

Americans have never solved our biggest problems by focusing on the small ones. Abolitionists did not end slavery by debating only whether slaves should be well fed, whether owners should keep slave families together, or whether slavery should expand to the territories. Those incremental issues were important, and concrete steps were taken to improve hundreds of thousands of lives.[19] But they were all done within the greater context that slavery itself was immoral and needed to be abolished—even at times when that seemed impossible.

There is no conflict between taking incremental steps to improve our elections and demanding we fix the fundamental damage that judicial ideologues have done to our Constitution. We can push for greater disclosure and public financing of campaigns, while simultaneously pushing for a constitutional amendment to overturn *Citizens United*.

What to Do—Step-by-Step Instructions

This book details how Americans have overcome incumbent self-interest and judicial activism before by passing amendments to our Constitution. There are particular lessons from the Seventeenth Amendment for direct election of US senators. We can also gain wisdom, and resolve, from the successful struggle to pass the Nineteenth Amendment for women's suffrage.

We will rediscover a process whereby voters gave specific marching orders, known as "voter instructions," to their elected representatives. Many of the delegates who met in Philadelphia to draft our Constitution did so under clear instructions from their constituents. Notably, those Framers specifically promised the people that they could use instructions to fix problems with the Constitution or the government it created through the amendment process. We can do the same today.

Voters in Montana, Colorado, and dozens of cities and towns have revived voter instructions and told their elected officials in no uncertain terms that they want a constitutional amendment to establish that unlimited campaign spending is not free speech. Unbelievably, the California Supreme Court blocked people from similarly speaking out by removing an instruction measure, Proposition 49, from the 2014 ballot.

When the court heard full arguments about the case on October 5, 2015, most justices appeared as though they were prepared to reverse their earlier rush to judgement and restore Proposition 49 to the ballot. A ruling is likely by January 2016, but as this book goes to print the court had not issued a final decision.

Working in parallel with the amendment process, we must also explore other avenues for overturning wrongheaded Supreme Court rulings. President Franklin D. Roosevelt faced a decade of disastrous rulings by the Supreme Court that struck down most of the New Deal. The court stood as an obstacle to rebuilding the American economy following the Great Depression. Although there were amendments introduced in Congress to overturn the rulings, Roosevelt found another way to elevate a constitutional crisis that roused a national conversation and forced the Court to reverse itself.

Throughout our history, there have been other examples, for good and for ill, of the executive and legislative branches pushing back on judicial interpretations and letting "We the People" serve as the final arbiters of our collective fate. It is, after all, "We the People" who adopted the Constitution and who are its sole source of legitimacy. We are not the ones who broke our democracy, but we are the ones who must fix it.

The hard truth is that it might take fifty to seventy years to reverse the Supreme Court's logic that unlimited campaign spending is free speech. The good news, which chapter 8 will detail, is that we are already forty years into that struggle and have made more progress than most people realize.

Whether by constitutional amendment or constitutional crisis, we have overcome seemingly "impossible" challenges to our republic before by conducting a national conversation of extraordinary proportion. We must set aside our differences on other matters and prioritize this crisis instead of sweating the small stuff. We do not have the time and energy to do this for every piece of bad news. But when we have confronted catastrophes in the past, Americans have time and again risen to the occasion.

The time has come for us to do so again.

Let's get to work.

What you can do: Join a group

You can't do this alone. See Appendix I for more than a dozen organizations that are working to overturn *Citizens United*. Join one. Better yet, join several.

PART 1 WHY WE MUST FIGHT

Chapter 1

Enough Is Enough

How and Why We Have Limited the Duration, Volume, and Location of Speech

I rise on behalf of the vast majority of the American people who believe money is not speech, corporations are not people, and government should not be for sale to the highest bidder. We demand that you overturn Citizens United.

—Kai Newkirk, addressing the Supreme Court, which promptly shut him up

The Supreme Court had never seen anything like it. On February 26, 2014, a young man in the audience stood up and had the temerity to speak his mind to all nine justices. The Court bailiffs promptly arrested Kai Newkirk—they silenced his speech so that other people could be heard. And they were right to do so.

The Supreme Court strictly regulates who is allowed to speak before the Court and how they must do it. It's not enough to be a lawyer. An attorney must be recognized as a special member of the bar of the Supreme Court of the United States. Attorneys must be nominated by another member of the bar and confirmed by the Court itself before they can utter a single word. Regular citizens are forbidden to speak.

Kai Newkirk was breaking all the Court's rules. He wasn't a lawyer and he wasn't representing anyone in the lawsuit before the Court. He was a visitor in the audience, which had been explicitly told it could not speak during the proceedings. Further, somebody videotaped Kai's speech and put it on the Internet—the first such incident in the history of a secretive chamber that prohibits any video recording of its proceedings.

Although court bailiffs were right to enforce the rules limiting speech in the Supreme Court chambers, Kai was surely right to speak out against the tyranny of a court that refuses to limit the paid speech of billionaires while telling Kai and the rest of us to shut up. In the *Citizens United* case, and many others, the Supreme Court has mistakenly held that limiting the money people and organizations can spend to purchase speech violates the First Amendment. In fact, our everyday experiences demonstrate that limiting each person's speech is necessary to ensure a full and free public debate. Let's consider some examples of how and why this is done.

Why We Limit the Duration of Speech

Courts impose strict page limits on the briefs that lawyers submit prior to hearings. Just ask the multinational oil company BP (formerly British Petroleum). During litigation surrounding its unprecedented oil spill in the Gulf of Mexico in

2010, the company submitted a brief that appeared to be within the thirty-five-page limit set by the court. However, district court judge Carl Barbier noticed that the company had slightly adjusted the spacing between lines to squeeze in the equivalent of six more pages than what was allowed. Judge Barbier warned that if BP continued such tactics, he would strike all future briefs from the company, saying "The Court should not have to waste its time policing such simple rules. . . . Counsel are expected to follow the Court's orders both in letter and in spirit."[20] If courts can limit corporate speech defending itself in litigation, why can't we limit corporate spending on elections that only indirectly affect corporate interests?

It is not just the city council in Richmond, California, or federal courts that limit how long a person can speak. We limit speech all the time. Turn on C-SPAN and you'll notice members of Congress pay close attention to just how much time they have to speak on the floor. They'll often ask the chairperson to allocate more time, or "yield back" the balance of their time to other members to speak. But if they exceed their time limit, the chairperson's gavel comes down, limiting their speech so that others may be heard. Similarly, during a debate for any office, from president down to state legislator, there are strict rules limiting the amount of time each candidate has for opening remarks and to answer each question.

Nobody seriously believes that these limits on the duration of certain political speech violate the First Amendment, which says that Congress shall not abridge the people's right to freedom of speech. In fact, these limits protect the First Amendment by ensuring that the people, and our representatives in Congress, can hear from opposing points of view and make informed decisions about self-government.

Why We Limit the Timing of Speech

My first summer job during college was going door-to-door on behalf of a grassroots campaign for an environmental organization. Police sometimes picked up canvassers on our team, telling them that door-to-door solicitation wasn't allowed in a particular community. It turns out they were wrong. Although courts have upheld bans on door-to-door solicitation for commercial purposes (such as the famed Fuller Brush man of long ago who knocked on doors selling cleaning supplies), the Supreme Court has specifically rejected bans on door-to-door solicitation for political speech.[21] Similarly, courts have upheld so-called "do not call" lists for commercial telemarketing even while allowing political campaigns to call voters uninvited. However, courts have upheld limits on the hours that you are allowed to knock on a person's door or call him on the phone—in many cities this is banned after nine o'clock at night. That limit on speech is justified because it balances the listener's right to privacy in his own home with your right to speak.

We also limit the timing of speech in public spaces. Just ask the activists of Occupy Wall Street. After holding signs and chanting "we . . . are . . . the 99 percent" for hours, the protesters decided to sleep in Zuccotti Park near Wall Street rather than heading home to the comfort of their beds. Other protesters joined them in solidarity in similar demonstrations across the country.

Months into the protests, police fell back on curfews as justification to storm the public parks and eject protesters using tear gas and sometimes violence. Thousands were jailed. In this way, police limited the duration of the protesters' speech by acting against alleged violations of the timing of that speech (in the form of curfews). This approach perhaps would have been reasonable if there were other people who wanted to use those same public spaces to speak about other issues, or even to simply enjoy some silence. But in this case, it's not clear that the protesters were preventing anyone else from speaking or disturbing the peace enough to lose their right to free speech, and the crackdowns were widely condemned.

How I Was Arrested for Speaking Too Much

In the summer of 2014, I joined Kai Newkirk and hundreds of others during the final day of a march on the California state capitol. Kai and others in the group 99Rise walked all the way from Los Angeles to Sacramento over thirty-seven days, enduring temperatures as high as 110 degrees in California's Central Valley.

March organizers had acquired a permit to protest on the steps of the capitol. But we wanted to continue our protest for longer than the permit allowed—long enough so that legislators would hear us when they came to their offices the following morning.

At 10:30 that evening, police informed us that our permit to protest had "expired"—as if there is an expiration date in the First Amendment. When we didn't leave, we were arrested, handcuffed, and taken to the county jail. The government had decided to limit the duration of our speech. It shut us up.

Had there been four other groups of people wanting to speak on the steps of the California state capitol at 10:30 that evening, then limiting our speech would have promoted First Amendment values. There are four sets of steps to the capitol—one on the east, west, north, and south. Occasionally, there are times when different groups are actually using each set of steps for a protest, press conference, concert, wedding, or other event. During those times, government permits enhance the ability of people to speak by ensuring that every group has a chance to use the limited forum of the capitol steps. The permits also prevent hecklers and other saboteurs from hijacking another group's event.

But if government limits on one person's speech are not enacted specifically to allow another person to speak, the limits don't further the First Amendment. Perhaps that is why the prosecutor declined to bring charges against me and the twelve other protesters who were detained that night.

This concept—that limitations on speech promote the aims of the First Amendment if they enhance the ability of other people to speak—is the core lesson we must apply to money in politics. The refusal to apply this simple principle is the Supreme Court's key failing.

Why We Limit the Volume of Speech

Besides limiting the duration and timing of speech, government also limits how loud we can be. In many states, it is illegal to drive a motorcycle that exceeds ninety-two decibels, even if the motorcycle is part of a political parade.[22] Some cities have ordinances that regulate amplified sound, even if it is coming from a political sound truck.[23] Your neighbors simply don't want to hear your views about abortion, war, or the minimum wage blasted at the volume of a rock-and-roll concert.

"This concept—that limitations on speech promote the aims of the First Amendment if they enhance the ability of other people to speak—is the core lesson we must apply to money in politics."

Police can arrest people for speaking too noisily. A dozen people from the Christ Fellowship Church were arrested for protesting too loudly outside a fund-raiser for a pro-gay marriage organization in North Carolina. Police claimed that the protesters were violating the city of Greensboro's noise ordinance.[24] If there were no limits on noise, anyone could silence speech they opposed by simply outshouting the speaker.

In addition to noise ordinances, most jurisdictions authorize police to arrest citizens for "disturbing the peace." Although this can be done for legitimate purposes, it can also quite literally mean that the government can shut you up when it thinks you should be quiet and peaceful. During protests across the United States in the wake of several police killings of unarmed African Americans in Ferguson, Missouri, and elsewhere, thousands of people were arrested for "disturbing the peace" because they were disrupting the normal flow of life in an attempt to make their views known.[25]

Police can and do silence protesters when they block traffic on highways or sidewalks, disturb shoppers, or otherwise make too much of a nuisance of themselves. Why? Because when one constitutional right conflicts with another right or interferes with our ability to govern ourselves, there's a legitimate reason to enforce limits. The principle at stake in the examples above is that one person's right to use her property (be it a motorcycle, a loudspeaker, or a protest sign) cannot violate another person's right to enjoy quiet on his own property or to drive down a highway unimpeded by protesters. When your freedoms trample on my liberties, we need to balance rights—including those espoused in the First Amendment.

Why We Limit the Location of Speech

Once when I was working on a campaign to increase recycling rates, some of the volunteers thought we should hold a large banner on a freeway overpass. Thousands of cars that drove below us would then see our message.

The highway patrol told us this was unsafe because motorists might be distracted by our political speech and could get into an accident. The government was limiting the location of our speech in order to protect the safety of motorists. That's a reasonable balance between First Amendment rights to free speech and the constitutional duty of government to promote the general welfare. It would be even more reasonable—and credible—if the government applied the same logic to billboards. Had the volunteers on my campaign been able to raise tens of thousands of dollars, we could have put the exact same banner on a billboard that the same motorists would have seen in a way that the highway patrol didn't view as distracting.

When more than ten thousand Tea Party activists descended on Washington, DC, in 2009 to protest the Affordable Care Act, ten of them were arrested for protesting inside the Capitol building. The police considered the protests "disorderly conduct" and quite literally silenced those protesters even while allowing many more to say the exact same thing outside the building.[26] Again it was the location, not the content, of the speech that the government was limiting.

Courts have similarly upheld limits on the location of speech outside polling places or abortion clinics. There is a legitimate question as to whether fifty feet, or five hundred feet, or five thousand feet is an appropriate balance between the free speech ideals of the First Amendment and the privacy rights of someone casting a vote or making an important decision without being harassed by someone screaming just inches away from her face. The challenge here is not whether there should be any limit on the speech, but what the limit should be.

Should We Ever Limit the Content of Speech?

Government rules on where we speak, when we speak, and how loudly we speak are less troubling than limits on what we say. Any regulation on the content of speech runs a great risk of limiting freedom of conscience and violating the First Amendment. But even when it comes to content regulation, many Americans agree some limits are justified.

Our government prohibits people from speaking about classified information that protects national security, for example. It is illegal to tell a foreign government, a terrorist organization, or even the general public information that could jeopardize the lives of Americans. Bradley Manning was sent to prison for revealing secret video footage that showed, among other things, US troop movements in Iraq.

Nonetheless, it is dangerous to allow the executive branch alone to decide what is secret and what is not. There is a difference between treason and legitimate whistleblowing or political dissent that presidents and their inner circle of advisors may not see in the fog of war. It is far too tempting for the government to label serious political opposition as jeopardizing national security. For instance, the administration of President Barack Obama attempted to ban the release of videos showing force-feeding of prisoners at the Guantanamo Bay detention facility, arguing it would harm national security because enemies of the United States might use the footage for propaganda. A judge disagreed with the notion that propaganda was a legitimate security threat and rejected the government's limit on the content of this speech.[27]

One of the reasons we need a judicial branch is to check the power of the executive branch. When President Richard Nixon tried to prosecute Daniel Ellsberg for leaking the

Pentagon Papers during the Vietnam War, a judge ultimately refused to convict Mr. Ellsberg. Ellsberg had violated government limits on his speech by giving classified documents to the *New York Times* for publication. But the judicial branch concluded that those restrictions were not justified by our national security interests. A jury might, or might not, come to a similar conclusion about Edward Snowden if he is ever brought to trial for violating limits on speaking about the National Security Agency's warrantless surveillance of American communications.

Some people believe there should be no government secrets. Projects such as WikiLeaks intentionally violate government limits on speech by leaking classified information to the news media and to citizens directly. But even WikiLeaks founder Julian Assange concedes that some information should be kept secret; he just believes that secrecy shouldn't be used to cover up government abuses.[28]

Whether or not you agree with Assange or Snowden, most Americans believe that at least some information should be classified. How to decide what types of speech to limit for national security purposes and what to make public is an important debate that is beyond the scope of this book. Nonetheless, even those citizens who think there should be absolutely no limits on the content of speech should think seriously about distinguishing that issue from whether we should limit the duration, timing, and location of speech— let alone the amount that billionaires may spend on political advertising. Similarly, we should separate the issue of regulating content of speech from limiting the amount of money that any person or group can spend to promote that speech in a political campaign.[29]

How Much Can One Person Hear?

Beyond legal limits on location, duration, volume, and even content of speech, the combination of our growing population and the information explosion of the past few decades has created an even more significant limit on everyone's speech—the limit on how much information each listener can absorb.

It is simply impossible for the president to listen to each and every one of the 320 million residents of the United States. A single member of Congress could not listen to everything that every constituent wanted to say, even if she spent all day doing nothing else. So, who will they listen to?

Here's how former senator Paul Simon put it: "In my last campaign, I spent $8.4 million running for reelection. It has a corrupting influence on all of us." Simon went on to explain what happens when he arrives at a hotel at midnight and finds twenty messages waiting for him, with nineteen from people he doesn't recognize and one from someone who has given him a $1,000 campaign contribution: "At midnight, I'm not going to make twenty phone calls. I might make one. Which one do you think I'm going to make?"[30]

Senator Bill Bradley was even more blunt: "Money not only determines who is elected, it determines who runs for office. Ultimately, it determines what government accomplishes—or fails to accomplish. Under the current system, Congress, except in unusual moments, will inevitably listen to the 900,000 Americans who give $200 or more to their campaigns ahead of the 259,600,000 who don't."[31]

Similarly, a voter does not have enough hours in the day to listen to everyone's opinions of how he should vote. Even if none of the government-imposed limits on time, place, and duration of speech existed, the real world imposes limits on how much any person can hear.

Yet if we want to govern ourselves thoughtfully and effectively, we need to hear various and opposing viewpoints about public policy options. So the question becomes: How do we decide which speech to listen to? And perhaps more importantly, who will choose?

Self-Government in an Age of Information Overload

At the founding of the United States, and indeed throughout most of world history, information was scarce. It simply wasn't possible to bombard citizens with more information than they could absorb. Limited technology, dispersed populations, and low literacy rates prevented the type of information overload we experience today.

In contrast, today's *New York Times* contains more information in a single issue than an ordinary citizen of the seventeenth century encountered during his entire lifetime.[32] Researchers estimate the average American consumes twelve hours of information a day.[33] This double-counts hours spent multitasking, such as checking e-mail while also listening to the news on television, but nonetheless the researchers estimate that we spend three-quarters of our waking time at home consuming some form of information. Yet try as we might, we can't come close to listening to everything that everyone has to say.

Behavioral scientists believe the average human brain can retain five to seven items in short-term memory.[34] Each additional piece of information above that physical limit quite literally displaces another piece of information in our brain. Speech competing for our attention, therefore, approaches a zero-sum game.

Marketing experts know that advertisements from one product, or one entire market sector, can crowd out advertisements for other products and sectors.[35] After a certain point, our brains become saturated and we start tuning out new ads for similar items.

Cognitive psychologist Herbert Simon tells us that

> *in an information-rich world, the wealth of information means a dearth of something else: a scarcity of whatever it is that information consumes. What information consumes is rather obvious: it consumes the attention of its recipients. Hence a wealth of information creates a poverty of attention and a need to allocate that attention efficiently among the overabundance of information sources that might consume it.*[36]

To deal with information overload, we limit what we pay attention to, including political speech.

When Less Is More: An Abundance of Limited Speech

This concept—that strict limits on speech enable more people to be heard—is the essence of the social networking service Twitter. By limiting each message to 140 characters, Twitter not only forces speakers to be concise but also allows listeners to follow the speech of hundreds, even thousands of fellow citizens.

Information sources recognized the need to limit speech long before the Internet age. Most newspapers impose strict word limits on letters to the editor, opinion columns, and even news stories by reporters. Just as there is only so much information that can fit in a person's brain, there is only so much news and opinion that can fit in a newspaper. In choosing which letters to print, opinion columns to carry, and news stories to cover, editors serve as information filters. They help readers decide which information is worth their time and which is not.

Because decisions about what speech to include involve political judgment, indeed a bias, it is important for readers to select news providers that they trust to limit speech in an appropriate and responsible manner. Self-government is best served when a citizen is exposed to differing political viewpoints, so most mainstream news editors provide an array of opposing views within one broad publication. Others provide information primarily from one political viewpoint. Both approaches are important and legitimate. What matters most is that readers know the biases, and ownership, of news outlets and can choose from a broad diversity of different news sources.

Social media, blogs, and the explosion of other online information sources have made it easier for citizens to create their own information filters. With Twitter and Facebook, you can decide who to "follow" and with blogs, you can choose which to read—you are not at the mercy of an editor. This opportunity to be our own editors offers incredible potential to expand political dialogue and engagement and reduce the concerns about powerful media conglomerates controlling which speech is heard and which is silenced.

Information expert Clay Shirky has noted that technology has already given us the tools we need to deal with the challenges of our information society. "There's no such thing as information overload," Shirky notes, "only filter failure."[37]

The ability to have filters with integrity has become key to our success as a nation.

Advertisements (which I'll explore as paid speech in the next chapter) cause filter failure. Advertisers selling products and services have information and opinions that no news editor would deem worthy of news coverage, so those advertisers pay the newspaper to run an ad. Advertisers who want to speak to people who are not following them on Twitter or Facebook can pay those companies a fee to have "sponsored" tweets or posts interrupt the information "feed" that the user has chosen to receive.

Advertising, by design, corrupts and distorts our marketplace of ideas—our chosen limits on speech. It takes the decision about which speech to include out of the hands of an editor (who the reader entrusts to play that role) and puts it into the hands of whoever has money to pay for it. Because we all have limited capacity to absorb speech, an advertiser not only pays to promote its own message but also to displace other speech that the listener might have listened to instead. Advertisements shut you up by drowning you out.

What you can do: Write the editor
Submit a brief letter to the editor of your local newspaper calling upon Congress to overturn the *Citizens United* ruling with a constitutional amendment. If they don't print it, get five friends to submit similar letters and see if one of you can break through the editor's filter.

Chapter 2

If Money Is Speech, Speech Is No Longer Free

The Difference between Paid Speech and Free Speech

Money is property. It is not speech.

—Supreme Court Justice
John Paul Stevens

Back in 1775, Thomas Paine had a problem. The revolutionary agitator needed to rouse American colonists into such fervor against England that they would declare independence and risk their lives in a war. But how could he get his message out across such a large territory? He couldn't have afforded TV ads even if they had existed at the time. Paine solved his problem by writing *Common Sense*, a 79-page pamphlet that swept through the colonies and solidified support for the American Revolution.

Campaign reform opponents have used Paine's pamphlet as an example of political speech that the British government would have censored if it could. They claim that campaign finance laws would have banned *Common Sense* and prevented the American Revolution.[38]

But here's where the critics are wrong. Paine *sold* his book. He wasn't paying for people to read his words—readers were paying to buy the book.[39] Although Paine gave away his copyright and donated his royalties to the revolutionary cause, *Common Sense* was not America's first political ad campaign. Rather, it was the most significant early use of the free press. It is that kind of free press that the Framers of our Constitution sought to preserve in the First Amendment, not political campaign advertising.

The Federalist Papers—Paid Speech?

When the Framers left the convention in Philadelphia with a draft of our Constitution and needed to persuade their fellow citizens to adopt it, they didn't launch an ad campaign. Rather, James Madison, Alexander Hamilton, and John Jay anonymously wrote a series of eighty-five articles that became known as *The Federalist Papers*. These writings have been used, quite correctly, as precedent for the importance of protecting anonymous speech.

However, *The Federalist Papers* do not justify anonymous campaign spending. That is because—just as with Thomas Paine's *Common Sense*—the articles were purchased by readers rather than foisted on them as paid advertisements. Under the title *The Federalist*, they were originally published in serial form in newspapers and then compiled into a booklet, which was also sold.[40] Although the authors were not attributed, readers could rely on the known reputations of the newspapers to evaluate the integrity of the writing.

The critical distinction in both instances is that while money was used to disseminate speech, the money didn't come from the person speaking.

The First Amendment and Campaign Ads

When Thomas Jefferson found the original Constitution faulty for failing to include a "bill of rights," he wrote:

> *There are rights which it is useless to surrender to the government, and which yet governments have always been fond to invade. These are the* rights of thinking, *and* publishing our thoughts *by speaking or writing.*[41]

Jefferson pushed James Madison to propose what became the first ten amendments to our Constitution. His writings make clear that Jefferson had in mind the freedom of conscience, to think what you want to think, as well as the freedom of the press, the ability to publish those thoughts, as critical components to self-government. There is no reason to believe Jefferson or other Framers were thinking about paid political advertisements when they drafted and ratified the First Amendment.

In fact, Jefferson and other Founders were deeply concerned about money distorting our government. Jefferson wrote that "of all the mischiefs, none is so afflicting and fatal to every honest hope as the corruption of the legislature."[42]

Decades earlier, in 1757, George Washington violated an ordinance in the colony of Virginia that forbid "treating" or giving "ticklers" to voters when he ran for the Virginia House of Burgesses. After losing his first race for office to a foe who provided free drinks to voters, Washington won his second election by purchasing more than a quart and a half of rum, wine, beer, and hard cider per voter in his district to distribute during the campaign.[43] After the United States won independence from Great Britain, several states enacted laws against treating, or bribing, voters directly and punished violators by removing them from office.[44]

It is clear our First Amendment protects freedom of speech, not freedom of spending. But there are genuine concerns about banning all spending of funds to discuss politics. It takes money to print the *New York Times*, just as it required funds to print *Common Sense* and *The Federalist Papers*. We need constitutional protections for spending money to publish political speech.

"Our First Amendment protects freedom of speech, not freedom of spending."

Justice John Paul Stevens has aptly described the difference between treating money exactly as free speech on the one hand and money as a legitimate means to disseminate speech on the other. Stevens noted:

> *Money is property. It is not speech. Speech has the power to inspire volunteers to perform a multitude of tasks on a campaign trail, on a battleground, or even on a football field. Money, meanwhile, has the power to pay hired laborers to perform the same tasks. It does not follow, however, that the First Amendment provides the same measure of protection to the use of money to accomplish such goals as it provides to the use of ideas to achieve the same results. . . .* The right to use one's own money to hire gladiators, or to fund "speech by proxy," certainly merits significant constitutional protection. *These property rights, however, are not entitled to the same protection as the right to say what one pleases.*[45] (emphasis added)

For instance, if spending money on political speech had no constitutional protections, could Congress ban someone from spending money to publish a book that advocated defeat of a presidential candidate? That's what Supreme Court Justice Samuel Alito asked Deputy Solicitor General Malcolm Stewart during the oral arguments for the *Citizens United* case: "You think that if a book was published, a campaign biography that was the functional equivalent of express advocacy, that could be banned?"[46]

Mr. Stewart got the answer wrong. He said while Congress couldn't ban the book, it could prevent corporations from paying to publish it.

What Stewart should have said was that a corporation could indeed publish the book if it then *sold it* to readers—that is the classic definition of the free press. But, if a corporation (or a billionaire for that matter) mailed unsolicited copies of a book-length political advertisement to thousands of voters right before an election, that would still be a campaign ad and subject to the same contribution limits and disclosure requirements that apply to all campaigns. Lengthening a two-page junk mailer into a book does not somehow magically convert a campaign flyer into the free press.

Where Is the Line between Paid Ads and the Free Press?

Stewart erred by falling into the trap set by reform opponents who intentionally conflate advertisements, or paid speech, with the free press that is sought out by listeners. Big money apologists use this trap repeatedly to make disingenuous arguments. Even the American Civil Liberties Union (ACLU) glosses over the distinction, saying "why would it be permissible for a major weekly news magazine to run an unlimited number of editorials opposing a candidate, but impermissible for the candidate or his supporters to raise or spend enough money to purchase advertisements in the same publication?"[47]

Kansas senator Pat Roberts explicitly conflated television programming and commercials during a 2014 Senate floor debate about a constitutional amendment to limit campaign spending. "Let's forget about the commercials just for a second," Roberts said. "Let's talk about the show."[48] But the show *is* entirely different from the ad, isn't it? People tune in to watch the show, not the ads.

During the same debate, Senator Ted Cruz went on to claim that allowing limits on political campaign spending would allow the government to jail the producers of political satire shows such as *Saturday Night Live*. Liberal megadonor Jonathan Soros (son of financier George Soros) has also suggested that limiting campaign spending could mean "monitoring the editorial power of the press."[49] Both claims are nonsense.

The constitutional amendment Senators Cruz and Roberts were debating specifically said, "Nothing in this article shall be construed to grant Congress or the States the power to abridge the freedom of the press." Instead of being absurdly inflammatory, Senators Cruz and Roberts could have raised a legitimate point. If we are going to allow limits on campaign spending but not allow limits on the free press, how are we to tell the difference? How can we draw bright lines between the two?

While common sense tells us that a TV show like *Saturday Night Live* would obviously fall within the free press, the text of the proposed amendment could provide for a more clear definition of what a press exemption meant. Chapter 7 will examine ways an amendment could do that.

Does Newsprint Make a Newspaper?

One fall day in 2012, Montana voters found what looked like a newspaper in their mailboxes called the *Montana Statesman*. The newsprint mailer had a headline reading, "Bullock admits failure: 1 in 4 sex offenders go unregistered." Steve Bullock, the attorney general who was viciously criticized in the article, was also running for governor. Montana law prohibits corporations from making political campaign contributions, but because this mailer looked like a "newspaper," the organization behind it claimed it could use corporate funds to print and distribute it and not even bother to disclose that fact. The group bragged to its potential donors (many of whom were oilmen and others from the extraction industry opposed to Bullock's candidacy) that "no politician, no bureaucrat, and no radical environmentalist will ever know you helped. The only thing we plan on reporting is our success to contributors like you."[50] Does printing a campaign ad on newsprint suddenly provide the constitutional protections of the free press? Of course not.

Previous campaign finance laws have attempted to define which news media outlets are exempt from campaign finance regulations based on the size of the circulation, how regularly it was printed or posted, or whether its staff were professional journalists as opposed to untrained volunteer bloggers. These definitions become complicated pretty quickly and can lead to the valid complaint that campaign finance laws make the rules about political speech too complex for ordinary citizens to follow.

Drawing the Line between Ads and the Free Press

Fortunately, there is a simpler solution. Rather than distinguishing the free press from campaign advertisements based on questions of content or means of production, we can draw a bright line based on whether the listener is paying to hear the speech (or otherwise actively soliciting the content) or whether somebody else is paying to present it to the listener. The *Montana Statesman* claimed it was the largest newspaper in the state because it was mailed to 120,000 people—but it didn't meet the standard of the free press because nobody actually subscribed to it. This distinction between unsolicited paid speech and solicited free speech resolves most of the confusion sown by the apologists of big money in politics.

We can draw a line between a newspaper story or editorial and a newspaper ad in the exact same publication. The essays comprising *The Federalist Papers* were written anonymously, but they were published as content in reputable newspapers that readers bought themselves, not as paid advertisements.

We can draw a line between a newspaper purchased by the reader at a newsstand and a big money political mailer (of any length) sent to the reader's doorstep unsolicited or distributed as a flyer on a street corner.[51] We can even extend this clear line to speech that the listener actively seeks out but does not pay for directly, such as when you check a book out of a library or tune into a news story on National Public Radio.

Senator Fritz Hollings, in response to a *Washington Post* editorial that opposed a constitutional amendment to limit campaign spending on the grounds it would violate free speech, retorted:

> *Go down to the* Washington Post *and say, "Now I want some of that free speech. I would like about a quarter page of that free speech, or a half page of that free speech you just editorialized about." And they will say, "Son, bug off. There is nothing free down here in this newspaper. You are going to have to pay for it, and you are going to have to pay for it under our rules and our regulations and our limits."*[52]

The line between paid speech and free speech holds for stories or programs that the reader receives for free but which are supported by distinct advertisements where advertisers do not control the content of the program, such as the case with most commercial radio and television programs, newspapers and magazines, and Internet news sites. But it is a different matter when an entire publication or program is subsidized by a funder who exercises editorial control. We can distinguish between an independent news program on a media outlet that deserves full First Amendment protection and a paid advertisement or program-length infomercial on the same outlet that does not. The distinction is not the form of speech but whether the reader seeks out the information (and pays for it directly with subscriptions or indirectly by tolerating discrete advertising) or is presented with unsolicited information from a paid bias.

Even with other types of Internet communications, the bright line between paid speech and free speech is easy to distinguish. It exists, for instance, between a paid Google search placement and the results of an organic search, or between a paid tweet and an authentic one.

The nonprofit organization Citizens United does a masterful job of conflating a documentary film, such as the one about Hillary Clinton at issue in the infamous *Citizens United v. Federal Election Commission* decision, and advertisements, which simultaneously promote the film and attack a candidate for office. One key flaw in the Supreme Court's *Citizens United* ruling was not that it allowed the organization to pay for the production costs of that movie from its corporate treasury, but that it failed to distinguish that legitimate free press function with the paid speech in the thirty-second ads aired by the same organization. Those ads should have been subject to campaign finance regulations even if the movie itself was not. Likewise, the $1.2 million that Citizens United paid a cable company to stream its movie for free, contrary to its normal pay-for-view programming rules, should have been treated as a campaign expenditure, whereas a similar $1.2 million paid by viewers to watch the movie under normal marketplace rules would not.

Similarly, the *New York Times*'s endorsement of candidates in its editorial columns is not a campaign ad because readers purchase the *Times* to read its content, including its editorials. But, if the *New York Times* bought TV ads during Monday Night Football to promote the candidates it had endorsed, those ads would be subject to the same campaign finance rules that apply to everyone. The New York Times Company is not exempt from campaign finance rules because it is in the news business, but sales of its newspaper are part of the free press because people subscribe to the

Times. This standard holds whether or not the *Times* (or any newspaper) operates as a corporation or just a group of unincorporated reporters and editors.

A Colorado court took more care than the Supreme Court in separating the free press aspects of a different Citizens United movie from the paid speech aspects of promoting that movie. In the case *Citizens United v. Gessler*, the Tenth Circuit Court ruled that the Citizens United organization must disclose the identity of the donors who paid for ads promoting a film that attacked Colorado governor John Hickenlooper, who was up for reelection when the ads were running. But, even though the organization looks more like a traditional political advocacy group than a news outlet, the court allowed Citizens United to pay for the movie's production cost with unlimited and undisclosed contributions.[53]

Limiting—Not Banning—Paid Speech

Even if we draw a bright line between speech that is paid for by the reader and advertisements funded by the speaker, we haven't completely resolved the issue. Speech on one side of the line, that which is solicited by the reader, deserves absolute First Amendment protection. Because there is no limit to the number of books a person can buy or number of movies she can watch, there should be no limits on selling books, newspapers, or movie tickets.

But ads are different. As Harvard law professor Paul Freund wrote:

> *Campaign contributors are operating vicariously through the power of their purse rather than through the power of their ideas. I would scale that relatively*

lower in the hierarchy of First Amendment values. Television ads have their value surely, and yet in terms of the philosophy of the First Amendment seem to be minimally the kind of speech or communication that is to be protected. We are dealing here not so much with the right of personal expression or even association, but with dollars and decibels. And just as the volume of sound may be limited by law so may the volume of dollars, without violating the First Amendment.[54]

Limits are different than a ban. As Justice Stevens noted, ads still deserve *some* protection. But because we have limited capacity to absorb information (as we discussed in chapter 1), everyone should decide for themselves what speech they want to hear and what they want to ignore. Thus, limits on campaign spending and advertising are justified to the extent that they enhance the ability of other opinions to be heard.

Those who benefit from unlimited campaign donations like to portray any limit on money in politics as a ban. But, limiting the amount that any deep-pocketed person or group can contribute toward airing a political ad does not ban the ad. It simply means that if the ad is going to be widely seen, many people will need to fund it or seek it out. Just as many people attending a city council meeting and each taking two minutes to make a point about the same topic will garner more attention than just one person speaking, campaign advertisements that represent the views of many small donors should garner more attention than those ads that represent the views of only one.

Similarly, requiring someone to pay for an ad using his or her own funds, rather than funds from a for-profit corporation, does not ban the ad. Corporate treasuries contain funds from many people who have invested for an economic purpose, not a political one. A corporate CEO, such as Chevron's John Watson, should not be able to use his investors' funds to promote his own political views or those of Chevron's board. When you make a decision to invest funds in a mutual fund or a 401(k) retirement account that holds stock in Chevron, you are not considering whether you want to support the candidates Chevron favors. You're just trying to save money for college or retirement.

Governments charter corporations and give them many privileges that individuals don't have for specific and important purposes—namely to promote large-scale economic enterprises. Using those privileges for other purposes distorts the corporate charter and the political marketplace.[55]

Removing the Junk with Information Filters

The same Richmond City Council meeting that limited the time each person could speak also discussed a proposal to reduce unwanted "junk mail." The council eventually adopted a program that allowed city residents to remove their names from direct-mail company lists in order to reduce the number of catalogs, flyers, and other advertisements they received. The goal was not only to cut down on wasted paper, but also to reduce the clutter in people's mailboxes—indeed the glut of information in our lives. While we rightly offer greater First Amendment protection to political mailers than we do to commercial mailers, the need to maintain some sort of information filters—to limit paid speech—remains paramount. This is the concept that we must clarify for our Supreme Court.

What you can do: Mute the ads

Hit the mute button during every political ad. Rather than relying on paid advertisements to inform you about candidates and ballot measures, do your own research. Subscribe to several news sources you trust and immediately throw any political mailers right in the recycling bin.

Chapter 3

Stupidity, Inequality, and Corruption

Three Good Reasons to Limit Paid Speech

The collective IQ of Congress goes down every two years.

—Chuck Todd

Imagine if you tried to make a difficult decision using only 4 percent of your brain capacity. You'd probably do some stupid things. Maybe you'd take up smoking cigarettes in an effort to improve your health. There was a myth for decades that we human beings actually use only 10 percent of our brains, but scientists have debunked that. A healthy person uses 100 percent of her brain—and even then we still make mistakes.[56]

Now imagine a society that only makes use of the collective wisdom of 4 percent of its citizens. Would that society make smart public policy decisions? That's what the Supreme Court has done by letting big money talk louder than the rest of us.

Roughly 4 percent of Americans contribute to a political campaign in any presidential year, but even that statistic grossly overstates participation. Most of the money comes from only the 0.2 to 0.4 percent of Americans who make a contribution of $200 or more to a federal candidate in each two-year election cycle, and this percentage has been shrinking over time.[57] If these are the only voices voters hear, we are missing out on the collective wisdom of 99.6 percent of Americans. That's a lot of speech that we aren't hearing.

We established in chapter 1 that there are limits to how much, how loudly, and in what locations we can speak with our voices, but also that these limits need to be justified by a very good reason. The limits need to balance free speech with other constitutional rights or principles of self-government. In chapter 2, I clarified that spending money to promote speech is different than speaking freely or publishing your thoughts for others to purchase. But chapter 2 also established that limits on spending money for political advertisements need to be justified by a good reason. In this chapter, we will explore three of those reasons: wisdom, which the Supreme Court hasn't thought about; equality, which the Court has rejected; and preventing corruption, which the Court has used disingenuously.

Reason #1: The Wisdom of the Crowd

The first good reason to limit money spent on political speech is to make wiser public policy choices. Political commentator Chuck Todd has said that the collective intelligence of Congress goes down every two years because smart people are deterred from running for office in the first place, in part due to the increasing role of big money in politics.[58] But the problem isn't just money impairing the collective wisdom of the 535 people we assemble in Congress to make decisions on our behalf. It's also the lost wisdom of the crowd that occurs when 82 million voters in the 2014 elections heard primarily from 124,522 donors who gave $2,600 or more to congressional candidates[59] when trying to set our national priorities through our elections process. If, as the old saying goes, two minds are better than one, surely hearing from 99.6 percent of voters is better than hearing only the opinions of 0.4 percent.

Academics who study information and knowledge development have noted that "in some cases, groups are remarkably intelligent and are often smarter than the smartest people in them."[60] Importantly, "the three conditions for a group to be intelligent are diversity, independence, and decentralization. The best decisions are a product of disagreement and contest. *Too much communication can make the group as a whole less intelligent.*"[61] Finally, they note that unless you limit the loudmouths, "groups may end up turning into mobs when diversity and independence are missing from the group."[62] (emphasis added)

When only 0.4 percent of the people are doing most of the talking, we are missing a great deal of diversity of thought. When elected officials listen primarily to those 0.4 percent who give the majority of campaign funds, their independence is severely compromised. Instead of a wise crowd, a foolish mob controls our government.

When More Isn't Better

Kansas senator Pat Roberts concludes that we need more money spent on campaigns by comparing those expenses to grocery items. "We spent more on yogurt in this year than we spent on political discourse, discussing the great issues of the day. . . . How much speech is enough? I submit we need more political speech, not less."[63]

But we are hungry for yogurt, not for attack ads. When voters are already saturated with information from 0.4 percent of Americans and lacking information from the other 99.6 percent, does it really make sense to allow those 0.4 percent to spend even more?

The ACLU has spent four decades telling legislators not to limit campaign spending. When legislators do enact limits, the ACLU asks judges to throw them out. The ACLU claims the solution to big money in politics is to add even more money to offset it.[64] It might sometimes make sense to fight fire with fire, as when firefighters set a small backfire to block the path of a raging forest fire. But the ACLU's position is akin to throwing a bucket of gasoline on your burning house instead of a bucket of water.

Rain is good during a drought, but in the middle of a flood more water is not what you need. And, make no mistake, the Supreme Court has opened the floodgates to big money campaign ads.

Likewise, if we can hold only so much information in our brains, does it make sense to saturate ourselves with a deluge of information from only a few perspectives? Or should we limit the amount any one person or group of people spends so that our brains can absorb a greater diversity of opinion?

Big money advertising doesn't only displace ideas and speech that voters seek out (the actual free speech that we should protect); the biggest money even displaces other ads. In hotly contested elections, TV and radio stations routinely run out of advertising space to sell to campaigns—so even those few *with* money can't buy speech. Ad space on websites targeting Republican voters in New Hampshire sold out eight months before the 2016 New Hampshire primary—before some candidates had even announced their campaigns.[65] At these levels of saturation, more speech is not even possible, let alone better.

It's the Money, Stupid: Public Policy and Tobacco

As an example of money in politics making us less wise, let's look at tobacco policy. For most of the twentieth century, tobacco use was the leading preventable cause of death in the United States. Even today, smoking-related health problems cost us $50 to $73 billion per year as a country.[66] Yet it took decades before we took serious steps to address this public health and economic disaster.

Early on, tobacco companies actually marketed cigarettes as beneficial to your health, for instance by suggesting they helped prevent obesity.[67] Then, from 1954 to 1999, the companies denied that cigarettes caused lung cancer, despite internal memos proving that tobacco executives knew otherwise.[68]

They flat-out lied through their teeth.

If Americans had access to a diversity of views, without the tobacco companies' money overwhelming the debate, public opinion and public policy would have moved quickly. But because information and speech was heavily unbalanced, we dithered—and millions died.

As our federal government gridlocked, many local officials who did not receive tobacco campaign contributions adopted bans on smoking in public places, and states enacted taxes on tobacco to fund prevention programs. Other policies restricted access by teens to tobacco and limited tobacco advertising and promotion—you could say we limited tobacco companies' speech promoting their products while we provided other speech to educate consumers about tobacco's negative health consequences.

These public policies decreased cigarette smoking by 33 percent from 2000 to 2011 while still preserving an individual's choice about whether to smoke and maintaining access to information about its pros and cons.[69]

Why did it take so long? Why were we so collectively stupid? Because big money from tobacco companies in the form of campaign contributions, lobbying, public relations, and funding of front groups and charities kept us from making wise decisions.

From 1986 to 1995, thirteen tobacco companies gave $9.9 million to federal candidates through their political committees.[70] These campaign contributions meant voters heard more from politicians who received those funds— even though the campaign ads rarely, if ever, discussed tobacco policy. In 1995, the 124 US representatives who opposed teen tobacco regulations received sixty-nine times more in campaign funds from tobacco interests than the 86 representatives who supported the regulations.[71]

Once elected, legislators heard from tobacco company lobbyists more than they heard from public health advocates who did not have campaign funds to buy access.

Campaign contributions also ensured that regulatory agencies heard from legislative recipients of tobacco money. For instance, three US senators who had received substantial campaign donations from tobacco companies sent a letter to the US Department of Health and Human Services that was copied almost word for word from a tobacco company memo faxed to the senators.[72]

In short, big money distorted who spoke, for how long, and how loudly. The skewed public dialogue led to skewed public policy that endangered people's health. It's no surprise that increased campaign money from the tobacco industry correlated with legislators taking weaker stands on tobacco control, according to a statistical analysis in six states.[73]

To Label, or Not to Label—That Is the Question

It is now accepted that cigarette smoking causes cancer, that tobacco companies knew this, and that they used their financial advantages to overpower the speech of opposing viewpoints that were pointing out the threats of tobacco to our health. But for issues we face today, we don't yet have the advantage of hindsight to know what ultimately will be viewed as the wise choice. The best we can do is ensure a balanced and fair debate.

Take the issue of using plants and animals in our food supply that have had their genes artificially manipulated. Some people believe this is wise because genetically modified organisms (GMOs) can produce more food per acre, resist disease and drought, and have greater nutritional value. Other people think it is unwise, at least until each GMO has been thoroughly tested to determine adverse effects on human health and on the greater ecosystem. Beyond any evidence, there is also an ethical question of whether humans should alter nature to such an extent.

One idea is to require GMO foods to be labeled so that consumers can choose whether they want to buy them. There are business interests on both sides, namely farmers who produce GMO-free food and those who grow food that has been modified. There are also public health, consumer, and environmental arguments on both sides.

But those two sides are not being equally presented.

A 2014 ballot initiative in Oregon to require labeling of GMO foods saw $10 million spent on the yes side but $20 million on the no side. The measure failed by fewer than a thousand votes. Prior to the onslaught of advertising in the campaign, the idea was polling at 77 percent support among Oregonians.[74]

Similar measures were defeated in California and Washington in 2012 and 2013 by nearly the same 51–49 margin. In Washington, the yes side spent $8 million and the no side spent $22 million—nearly three times as much. In California, the no side spent $47 million, outspending the yes side's $8.7 million by more than five to one. The results suggest industry campaign consultants use precise polling to know just how much they must spend to defeat a measure. A year after the 2013 defeat in Washington, support for the idea was back up to 69 percent. Once the advertising stopped, public opinion reverted to where it had been.

Regardless of whether you think GMO foods should be labeled, can any of us be confident that the "wise" public policy outcome was achieved in any of these three ballot measures when the political speech was so imbalanced? If each side had spent the same amount of money, or if each individual donor had only been allowed to contribute a maximum amount, would the results have been different? Should public policy be determined by money or by fair debate?

The wisdom of the crowd, our very ability to govern ourselves smartly, has been compromised by a flood of big money unleashed by foolish decisions from the Supreme Court. Reducing our collective stupidity is a very good reason to limit the amounts of money that wealthy donors spend drowning out the diversity of voices in America.

Reason #2: Reducing Political Inequality

The wealthiest 0.1 percent of Americans now control a greater portion of our nation's wealth than at any time since the Great Depression. This growing concentration of wealth in the hands of the few threatens both our economy and our democracy.

Nine times out of ten, the candidate for Congress who raises the most money wins the election. Knowing this, candidates spend their time talking to rich people and asking them for big chunks of money, leaving little time to talk to average people who might only be able to give $25 or $50. In the 2010 election cycle, 26,783 people donated more than $10,000—the total amount these individuals donated represented one-fourth of all the funds raised by candidates, parties, and political committees.[75] Over half of these donors were tied to corporations, and 15 percent were either lobbyists or lawyers.[76] These donors live primarily on the coasts or in such major cities as Chicago and Dallas, yet they give primarily to candidates outside the districts they live in.

In the 2014 campaign cycle, the top one hundred donors contributed nearly as much as an estimated 4.75 million people who gave $200 or less to a federal candidate.[77] So, each of those plutocrats had nearly five thousand times as much influence as the average small donor.

The Rich *Are* Different

This sort of political inequality creates at least two major problems.

First, candidates who are most successful at raising money from wealthy people and interests are the ones most likely to win. This reality skews the pool of candidates who choose to run for office in the first place,[78] since not everyone interested in politics is willing or able to play the money game. Moreover, even if the donors had absolutely no influence on the opinions of candidates they support, we wind up with a Congress that is more likely to reflect the views of the wealthy than of ordinary Americans because candidates with views the wealthy approve of will win.

If wealthy Americans had the same viewpoints as average Americans, their supersized influence would not distort our public dialogue or our elections. But wealthy Americans do not have the same viewpoints as ordinary folks. The day-to-day experiences of wealthy people are dramatically different from most people. One study found that wealthy people worried far more about federal budget deficits than average people, who were more concerned about unemployment.[79] While a majority of Americans favored increasing taxes on millionaires as a way to reduce the deficit, wealthy survey respondents, not surprisingly, didn't think that was such a good idea.[80]

The second problem comes from candidates having hundreds of conversations with wealthy people in the process of asking them for money. These conversations *do* have an influence on the opinions and priorities of the candidates and those who then get elected. That is, after all, the whole point. When Charles Keating, the CEO of the Lincoln Savings and Loan Association at the heart of the 1980s S&L crisis, was asked if his political contributions had worked to influence legislators to take up his cause, he replied, "I want to say in the most forceful way I can: I certainly hope so."[81]

It cost US taxpayers $3 billion to bail out the savings and loan industry after reckless behavior by Keating and others, which was only allowed due to loosened regulations.[82] It cost Keating only a few pennies on the dollar in campaign contributions to buy the influence he needed to keep his fraudulent banking practices going. One regulator described a meeting with the so-called Keating Five, a group of US senators that Keating had plied with $1.3 million in campaign contributions, as "tantamount to an attempt to subvert the regulatory process."[83]

Donors know when they speak with a candidate, either directly or through a hired lobbyist, that speech is persuasive. It may not always convince the candidate toward the donor's point of view, but it is more beneficial to the donor to have the conversation than to not. Their donation buys access and influence with elected officials, which is why they write the check. Money talks.

When a tiny group of wealthy people have dramatically more influence over who runs for office, who wins elections, what issues candidates campaign on, what issues they discuss privately with donors and regulators, and how they officially act upon those issues while in office, we have lost the core principle in a democracy of one person, one vote.

Majority Rule or Oligarchy?

The American Revolution was fought to abandon the rule of monarchy and the outworn concept of the divine right of kings. The Declaration of Independence eloquently established that the sole justification for a democratic government's authority is that it rules by consent of the governed. This doesn't mean everyone agrees with every law, but a majority of citizens should.

For a governing majority to be legitimate, it must be a majority of citizens who each have an equal say.

An oligarchy does not operate by majority rule. Rather, an elite group rules by force, manipulation, or deceit.

Although modern Russia goes through the motions of conducting elections, the centralized control of the media, business, and political party apparatus in the hands of a small elite has led many to conclude that Russia is an oligarchy, not a democracy.

"For a governing majority to be legitimate, it must be a majority of citizens who each have an equal say."

So elections, on their own, do not guarantee a democratic republic.

But what about the United States? Are we really a democratic republic that derives its authority from majority consent of the governed?

As far back as 1994, three-quarters of survey respondents agreed that "our present system of government is democratic in name only."[84] Perceptions aside, the problem has been getting worse over time as measured statistically. Using statistical analysis comparing the votes of legislators with the wishes of both constituents and extremely wealthy people, a researcher from Princeton found that economic elites and business interests have "substantial" impact on government policy in the United States while average citizens have "essentially no impact."[85] Similar academic research has found that Congress followed the wishes of the majority of Americans 40 percent of the time in 2000, which was down from about two-thirds of the time in 1980.[86]

We are conducting elections, but not under conditions that allow for a diversity of viewpoints and opposition to be heard. In other words, the United States now more closely resembles an oligarchy, where the wealthy minority rules, than a representative democracy of one person, one vote.

Reason #3: Reducing Corruption

A third reason to limit money in politics, and the only reason that the Supreme Court acknowledges, is to prevent corruption. The trouble is, the word "corruption" means different things to different people.

When we say that a computer file has been corrupted, we mean that it no longer contains its true content. The integrity of the information in the file or program has been distorted and it needs to be restored to its original form in order to function properly.

If Americans observed an election where ballot boxes were stuffed with multiple fake ballots or candidates from opposition political parties were jailed to prevent them from speaking out, we would consider those elections corrupt and lacking legitimacy. The true intent of the electorate would not be accurately expressed through such a corrupt voting system.

The *Merriam-Webster Dictionary* offers four definitions of corruption:

1. impairment of integrity, virtue, or moral principle: depravity

2. decay, decomposition

3. inducement to wrong by improper or unlawful means (as bribery)

4. a departure from the original or from what is pure or correct [87]

For five members of the Roberts Court, corruption means only the third definition: explicit bribery. If somebody offers a government official money on the condition that the official takes some action in return, that is one type of corruption. The legal world calls this "quid pro quo" corruption, using fancy Latin words meaning "something for something."[88]

Some legislators want campaign funds so badly that they are willing to essentially sell votes and favors to donors with vested interests in order to secure them. Because of the very real chance of succeeding with this bribery form of corruption, the Supreme Court agrees we can limit the amount of money given directly to a candidate.

A Narrow Definition Makes for a Thin Veil

The first flaw with the Roberts Court's extremely narrow definition of corruption is that it mistakes quid pro quo agreements as the principle culprit when in fact the problem is unequal influence.[89]

There may be nothing wrong with quid pro quo behavior if no money changes hands—indeed Americans fully expect politicians to make explicit agreements with us all the time. They are called campaign promises. We agree to vote for a candidate who promises not to raise our taxes, or to end a war, or to create jobs. This is what allows voters to hold legislators accountable when they violate a campaign promise. However, everyone can barter their vote for a campaign promise, but only a few can write a thousand dollar check. It is the unequal chance to swap money for votes that corrupts politics, not the fact that there is an exchange.

Further, limiting the size of a contribution does not prohibit all quid pro quo behavior. Big donations could come with no strings attached simply because the donor agrees with the publicly stated positions of the candidate. Conversely, donors can and do receive small favors in exchange for smaller contributions. One common perk is for an elected official to take a picture with a donor in exchange for a specific campaign donation. The donor then hangs the photo on his office wall and signals prospective business partners that he has political access and legitimacy. But if you can bundle lots of thousand dollar checks for a candidate, you can bargain for a lot more than just a photo.

Legislators can provide favors without an explicit agreement, often in ways that are impossible for the public to detect. Senator William Proxmire observed, "The payoff may be as obvious and overt as a floor vote in favor of the contributor's desired tax loophole or appropriation. Or it may be subtle . . . a floor speech not delivered . . . a bill pigeonholed in subcommittee . . . an amendment not offered . . . Or the payoff can come in a private conversation with four or five key colleagues in the privacy of the cloakroom."[90]

Another flaw in defining corruption only as explicit deal making is that it leads to a system of "wink and nod" influence peddling. Here's how Alan Robbins, a California legislator who served two years in prison for political corruption, described it:

> *What goes on . . . in Sacramento is that the . . . lobbyist comes in and on Monday he talks to you about how he's arranging for a campaign contribution to come from his client, and on Tuesday he comes back and asks you to vote on a piece of legislation for that same client. It doesn't take very long before the least-bright legislator figures out that if he keeps ignoring the Tuesday request then the lobbyist is going to stop coming to his fund-raisers. And, especially when you talk about a*

*lobbyist who controls over $1 million a year of cam-
paign money, who can make or break one's career, it's
very easy for legislators to come to the conclusion that
his arguments are persuasive.*[91]

Chief Justice John Roberts and the four others who joined
in the *Citizens United* decision (the "Roberts Five") have made
a mockery of even their own narrow definition of corruption
by claiming it is absolutely impossible to corrupt a legislator
with a huge contribution to a political campaign that somebody else runs for the candidate's benefit. For instance, the
Citizens United ruling implies it could be corrupting for Florida ophthalmologist Salomon Melgen to give $2,701 directly
to Senator Bob Menendez's campaign, but not corrupting for
Melgen's company to give $600,000 to a super PAC campaign
fund to spend on Menendez's reelection.

It's unclear that anybody beyond those five members of
the Roberts Court actually believes this to be true,[92] and you
have to wonder if even they believe we can't see through the
thin veil they are using to cover legalized bribery. They came
to this conclusion without a shred of evidence. As chapter 4
will discuss, this constricted definition of corruption is what
led to the creation of the so-called super PACs in the 2012
election cycle, which accepted unlimited campaign contributions and rendered the previous contribution limits
meaningless.

A final flaw in the Roberts Five bribery definition of corruption is that it focuses only on a legislator's actions and decisions, not on the need for voters to make informed decisions
based on having access to balanced and diverse viewpoints.
The "corruption only as bribery" perspective adopts an elitist
view of government. Elitists presume the legislator's job is to

act as an expert to solve difficult problems regular voters are too stupid to figure out. A more populist view presumes that the elected official's job is to represent the collective wisdom of her constituents, who are, after all, the ones in charge.

This popular view of representation actually *depends* upon a quid pro quo type of agreement where the elected official agrees to do what her constituents tell her to do. When you think about representation this way, big money campaign ads only serve to distort the wisdom of the crowd and corrupt the political process regardless of whether the money passes through a candidate's hands.

Three Ways of Saying the Same Thing

In this chapter, I have listed three perfectly good reasons to limit paid speech—protecting the wisdom of the crowd, reducing inequality, and combating corruption—but arguably they are all the same thing. Our public policy-making process is corrupted because big money gives unequal influence to a tiny group of people who distort the wisdom of the crowd and the wisdom of elected officials that would otherwise be achieved if everyone had an equal chance to be heard. When money talks, democracy suffers.

Any one of these approaches to looking at the problem justifies limits on the amount of money any one person or group spends on political campaigns or advertisements. These reasons also can guide courts in determining what sorts of laws are contrary to our First Amendment, namely those laws that give a tiny and unrepresentative group of people unequal and undue influence. Our courts should be questioning the constitutionality of our current system of unlimited campaign spending, not striking down every effort to level the playing field and ensure a diversity of opinions.

What you can do: Send 'em speech

When the ACLU, or any politician, sends you a letter asking for your money, send them back some speech instead. Simply write your opinion about their stance on *Citizens United* and mail it back in the return envelope they conveniently provide.

Chapter 4

Who Broke Our Democracy?
How Courts Have Struck Down Limits on Money in Politics

The concept that government may restrict the speech of some elements of our society in order to enhance the relative voice of others is wholly foreign to the first amendment.
— US Supreme Court, *Buckley v. Valeo*, 1976

If money is speech, as the Supreme Court says, then more money must be more persuasive speech, and those ideas with the most money behind them will tend to prevail. This is un-American.
— US Senator Barbara Boxer

When Senator James Buckley lost a political battle on the floor of the Senate in 1974, he didn't get mad. He got even.

Senator Buckley strongly opposed the new campaign finance rules passed by Congress in the wake of Watergate. When President Gerald Ford signed the Federal Election Campaign Act (FECA) of 1974 into law, Buckley followed a great American tradition of sore losers.

He sued.

But before telling that story, let's first meet James Buckley.

Who Is James Buckley?

James Buckley inherited a small fortune as part of his family's oil and gas services company, Catawba, in 1958. His father, William F. Buckley Sr., founded Catawba to exploit oil and mineral rights in Venezuela and Mexico. Like oilman Fred Koch, who passed on extreme wealth and extreme politics to his sons Charles and David, Bill Buckley Sr. was heavily invested in politics as well as oil and gas. James ran for the US Senate from New York in 1968 at the urging of his well-known brother, columnist William F. Buckley Jr. Running as a member of the Conservative Party, a marginal player in New York politics, he spent little money and received 16 percent of the vote.

Buckley tried again as a Conservative Party candidate in 1970 against a sitting Republican incumbent. During a televised debate, he agreed that campaign spending should be limited,[93] and yet he spent $1.8 million on his campaign—a huge sum at the time. James Buckley won the three-way race with 38 percent of the vote.

After the Watergate reforms, Buckley reversed his public support for campaign spending limits. Instead of backing spending limits as he had promised, Buckley personally went to court to void the law his colleagues had just passed.

Political extremes on the left and the right joined Buckley in the lawsuit, including the liberal Eugene McCarthy, the Socialist Labor and Socialist Workers parties, the American Conservative Union, and the American Civil Liberties Union (ACLU). The case became known as *Buckley v. Valeo*, legally pitting Buckley against Francis R. "Frank" Valeo, the clerk of the Senate. Although he won in court, Buckley lost his reelection campaign in 1976 as well as a

1980 Senate race in Connecticut. After losing decisively in the arenas of public opinion and elections, James Buckley received a lifetime appointment as a federal judge from President Ronald Reagan in 1985.

Court Rulings before *Buckley*

For nearly two hundred years of US history, judges had not significantly meddled with campaign finance law. State and federal laws limiting campaign spending had been on the books for more than seventy-five years prior to *Buckley* with little litigation.

The First Amendment did not suffer during that time.

In 1898, the Ohio Supreme Court upheld campaign spending limits and removed John Mason from office for violating the limits.[94] In 1921, Truman Newberry was convicted for violating campaign spending limits during his 1918 race for the US Senate. The US Supreme Court overturned his conviction in the case *Newberry v. United States*, which held that Congress could limit spending in general elections but not during primaries and party nominations because those were private affairs.[95] But the Court reversed this ruling in 1941 in the case *United States v. Classic*.[96]

Congress passed new limits in 1925 for general election campaigns by amending the Corrupt Practices Act. These limits were not struck down by the courts, but they also were not enforced by the executive branch.

Facts Be Damned—but Lower Courts Uphold the Law

After the Watergate scandal, Congress enacted tough new limits on campaign contributions and spending.[97] To ensure the new law would be in effect for the 1976 elections,

Congress included a provision proposed by Senator Buckley for expedited legal review.

Normally a law must take effect before somebody can challenge it in court, so that there is a track record of how the law actually works for the court to consider. Not in this case. Lawyers simply fabricated claims about how they expected the law would work.

On January 24, 1975, US district court judge Howard Corcoran certified the constitutional questions involved in the case without making any effort to ascertain any facts. On August 15, an eight-judge panel of the US Court of Appeals upheld almost all of the law.[98] The court's logic was straightforward:

The power of Congress to regulate federal elections embraces, in our view, the power to adopt per candidate and overall limitations on the amount that an individual or political committee may contribute in the contest of federal elections and primaries.[99]

The court noted that the problem of money in politics had grown so substantial that "the situation not only must not be allowed to deteriorate further, but that the present situation cannot be tolerated by a government that professes to be a democracy."

Given the additional deterioration since then, where does that leave our democracy now?

The appeals court concluded by noting that the new law's provisions "should not be rejected because they might have some incidental, not clearly defined effect on First Amendment freedoms. To do so might be Aesopian in the sense of the dog losing his bone going after its deceptively larger reflection in the water."[100]

The US Supreme Court wasted no time in dropping the bone.

Supremely Unusual Proceedings

The Supreme Court issued its final ruling on January 30, 1976, with campaigns already underway for November. Contrary to Court custom, no justice signed the *Buckley* opinion.

Perhaps nobody wanted to take responsibility for it. Multiple authors drafted it, most likely Justices William Brennan, Potter Stewart, and Lewis Powell, who were the only three who agreed with the entire opinion. Powell had been put on the court by President Nixon shortly after writing a secret memo describing how business interests needed to take over the judiciary.[101] Stewart was a centrist. Brennan was one of the Court's leading liberals.

It is quite possible Justice Brennan later regretted his part in the ruling, as the legal think tank founded in his honor by his former clerks made overturning the *Buckley* ruling one of its first priorities.[102]

In the *Buckley* ruling, each justice had his own dramatically differing view about what the First Amendment says. Some justices saw the word "money" in the First Amendment—perhaps written in invisible ink because others did not see it there. There were multiple dissents and concurring opinions, which allow us to see how the votes broke down regarding the different pieces of FECA.

Six justices supported the limits on contributions from donors to candidates, while seven opposed the overall limits on what a candidate could spend. You might think that when the members of the Supreme Court cannot agree amongst themselves about what the Constitution says, they would defer to people who know much more about political campaigns than they do—like legislators. Instead, the justices thought they knew better than everyone else.

Mistake #1: Money = Speech

As the centerpiece of its 76,000-word opinion in *Buckley v. Valeo* (the longest in Court history), the Supreme Court majority argued that spending money to disseminate speech is the same thing as the First Amendment freedom of conscience and the ability to publish one's thoughts through the free press. This, the Court said, is because "virtually every means of communicating ideas in today's mass society requires the expenditure of money."[103]

While this is mostly true, *Buckley* wrongly assumes that the speaker must spend the money to convey an idea, not the listener.

Perhaps because it was so rushed to issue an opinion, or perhaps simply because different justices asserted their own personal ideologies, the *Buckley* court fundamentally conflated free speech with paid speech. Whether by accident or design, the Court ignored the distinctions I've drawn in chapter 2.

Judge Skelly Wright, one of the lower-court appellate judges who upheld the law, understood the difference between paid speech and free speech. He later observed, "The Court told us, in effect, that money is speech. . . . [This view] accepts without question elaborate mass media campaigns that have made political communications expensive, but at the same time remote, disembodied, [and] occasionally . . . manipulative. Nothing in the First Amendment . . . commits us to the dogma that money is speech."[104]

Misreading King Solomon, the Court Splits the Baby

King Solomon famously found the truth when two women quarreled over who was the real mother of an infant. After saying the baby should be split in two, he noticed that the real mother immediately gave up her claim in order to save the child's life. Solomon then gave the baby, unharmed, to her.

When members of the Supreme Court quarreled about whether the post-Watergate limits on money in politics voided the First Amendment, they gave up on the truth. Instead, they actually split the baby, handing back only half a law to Americans.

To negotiate a compromise that a majority on the court could support, the *Buckley* ruling upheld campaign contribution limits but removed the spending limits that were central to the law's success. In doing so, it effectively destroyed the efforts of citizens and Congress to reclaim our democracy and our liberty for the next forty years. That's something no foreign invader or terrorist has ever managed to do.

The logic of *Buckley* barely held together at the time: How could money sometimes be speech and sometimes not? It has since been ridiculed by both supporters and opponents of campaign finance reform.

Only four justices agreed with treating contributions and spending differently. A fifth, Justice Thurgood Marshall, agreed in principle but thought that a candidate's contributions, such as Donald Trump's, to his own campaign should be limited.[105] Chief Justice Warren Burger understood that half of a baby will not survive, saying prophetically, "The Court's attempt to distinguish the communication inherent in political contributions from the speech aspects of political expenditures simply will not wash. . . . The Court's result does violence to the intent of Congress." He was right.

The Court's Untenable Justification

The *Buckley* court then needed to justify its compromise. Money was always speech, *Buckley* inferred, but some reasons to limit speech were very good and others just weren't good enough.

The Court concocted a twisted, narrow definition of corruption (discussed in chapter 3) as an explicit agreement to trade a campaign contribution for a government favor. This risk of bribery meant that there was a good reason for contribution limits. The *Buckley* opinion then noted there was no chance that candidates could bribe themselves, so limits on how much personal wealth a candidate could spend were rejected.

Buckley went on to void all candidate campaign spending limits, reasoning that nobody is bribed just because somebody spends five times as much as somebody else to disseminate one viewpoint.

The *Buckley* opinion went out of its way to reject political equality as a good reason for spending limits—even though we enforce equal time requirements in town halls, on the floors of Congress, and even within the Supreme Court itself. To explain themselves, *Buckley*'s anonymous authors made up a bald-faced assertion:

> *The concept that government may restrict the speech of some elements of our society in order to enhance the relative voice of others is wholly foreign to the First Amendment, which was designed to secure the widest*

*possible dissemination of information from diverse and
antagonistic sources and to assure unfettered inter-
change of ideas for the bringing about of political and
social changes desired by the people.*[106]

Buckley was correct on the goals of the First Amendment
but flat-out wrong that limiting campaign spending doesn't
further those goals. In fact, as chapter 1 discussed, spending
limits allow the widest possible dissemination of information
from diverse and opposing sources. By equating campaign
spending with free speech and then ignoring the reasons to
limit that spending, the Court's decision opened the floodgates to corruption, inequality, and foolishness in politics.

Is Corruption in the Eye of the Beholder?

Beyond its narrow definition of quid pro quo corruption to
justify limits on campaign contributions, the court added
another broader reason: the "appearance" of corruption. In
other words, we don't have to know for sure that each and
every campaign contribution leads to a specific bribe; we
can limit campaign contributions if overall a system of large
contributions undermines people's faith in our government.

It sounds okay on the surface, but this rationale of limiting money in politics whenever it "appears" corrupting has
proven to be a can of worms.

The problem is, as we discussed in chapter 3, different
people have different definitions of corruption. We now have
the Roberts Court telling the citizens of the United States
that we do not get to decide for ourselves what appears corrupting to our own eyes. Rather, five unelected judges who
have zero experience with political campaigns will substitute
their judgment for ours.

Corporations Become People—
Long Before *Citizens United*

Striking down half of the post-Watergate campaign finance law was only the beginning of *Buckley's* tyranny.

Two years later, the Supreme Court used *Buckley's* twisted logic to destroy a Massachusetts Corrupt Practices Act provision from the early 1900s that the legislature had recently updated. The law banned CEOs from using shareholder funds for candidate and ballot measure campaigns. As with *Buckley*, lower courts upheld the law and the Massachusetts Supreme Court found it constitutional.

A majority on the US Supreme Court disagreed.

The *First National Bank of Boston v. Bellotti* opinion, written by Justice Lewis Powell, a former corporate lawyer, claimed that for-profit corporations were to be treated as people under the Fourteenth Amendment. That amendment, meant to protect the rights of former slaves, guaranteed equal protection of the law to all people. Powell went on to argue that "the inherent worth of the speech in terms of its capacity for informing the public does not depend upon the identity of its source, whether corporation, association, union, or individual."[107]

Tell that to Kai Newkirk, who John Roberts had arrested for speaking without permission. The Supreme Court finds no value in the speech of real people if they are not members of the Supreme Court bar association—their speech has no inherent worth based on their identity.

The *Bellotti* ruling to allow unlimited corporate spending in ballot measure campaigns split the court along a controversial 5–4 vote—a sure sign that so-called constitutional experts can disagree about what is corrupting even while citizens largely agree. Conservative justice William Rehnquist dissented, noting that the Court should not ignore the consensus of the federal government and thirty state governments that had banned corporate money from being used in elections.

Ballot Measures Go Up for Auction

A few years later, in 1981, lower courts extended the logic in *Bellotti* and struck down a local ordinance in California that limited real people's contributions to ballot measure campaigns. The court reasoned that because no elected officials are involved in ballot questions, there was nobody to bribe and therefore no reason to limit campaign money.

Of course, there *were* reasons other than bribery, such as ensuring the wisdom of the crowd by hearing from all sides of the issue. But the courts didn't want to hear about those reasons. As a result, the citizen initiative process in California and twenty-three other states has become overwhelmed with big money.

It's ironic that a tool that was created a hundred years ago to help citizens take back control from corrupt legislatures has been converted into a tool for corporations and billionaires to parade their ideas before voters. Clever candidates have begun using ballot measure campaigns as a way to circumvent contribution limits on their own campaigns—they can accept unlimited donations to put themselves in TV ads so long as they talk about the ballot measure instead of their own election.

The Other Shoe Drops as Courts Gut Contribution Limits

Although the *Buckley v. Valeo* ruling did uphold the federal limit of $1,000 on contributions to candidates, that limit was so high at the time it restricted very few donations. It was a bit like upholding a 200-mile-per-hour speed limit—only a few cars can go that fast anyhow.

When voters in the 1990s began passing state and local voter initiatives that limited contributions to amounts that were within striking distance of what many Americans could afford, some judges balked.

In 1995, a federal appellate court overturned a lower court ruling and struck down Missouri's Proposition A, which 74 percent of voters passed to limit legislative contributions to $100. The court left in place slightly higher contribution limits enacted by the legislature, which would again be challenged five years later, in a case known as *Nixon v. Shrink Missouri Government PAC*.

In 1996, a federal court overseeing the District of Columbia struck down the low contribution limits that had been approved by voters four years earlier. The court noticed that the limits reduced overall spending by candidates who couldn't raise as much money as they had previously.[108] Therefore, the court thought the contribution limits acted in fact as a spending limit.

The DC court noted that while *Buckley* had allowed for limits on contributions, those were *only* okay because they were so high that only 5 percent of contributions had previously been over that limit. We'll never know if higher courts would have agreed with the local judge because the incumbents on the city council took the opportunity to gut the initiative that voters had approved and put in place much higher limits.

In 1997, the Oregon Supreme Court also struck down low contribution limits passed in Measure 9, after the law had been in place for one election cycle. The court didn't care that 72 percent of Oregonians thought that limiting the paid speech of each person would allow more people to be heard and reduce the "undue influence" of wealthy donors. The Oregon court didn't even bother with a trial to examine evidence as to how the law had worked in practice. The judges simply decided they knew better than Oregonians did about how they should govern themselves.

The judicial assault on democracy kept rolling. In 1998, California district judge Lawrence Karlton struck down Proposition 208, passed by voters in 1996 to set contribution limits of $250 for legislative candidates. As in the District of Columbia, when it appeared likely Karlton's ruling would be reversed upon appeal, the California legislature moved to enact much higher contribution limits, deceptively telling voters that they were better than nothing.

The "Can't Vote, Can't Contribute" Rule

Imagine if citizens in a New England town meeting had to listen while out-of-state lobbyists talked for hours until everyone had to go home. They'd never allow it.

Or imagine if foreign nations or corporations could spend unlimited amounts to influence US elections. That's wrong—outsiders shouldn't be spending money to influence elections they cannot vote in.

Well, in 1996, a federal court struck down Oregon's Measure 6, which prevented candidates from accepting contributions from people who lived outside the candidate's district. The court found the "can't vote, can't contribute" rule a violation of the First Amendment. Using *Buckley*'s strained logic, the court said contributions from outside the district weren't any more likely to bribe a legislator than contributions from within the district, therefore they must be allowed. Only one judge disagreed, saying "states have a strong interest in making sure that elections are decided by those who vote."[109]

The Supreme Court of Alaska took a different view on out-of-state campaign money. That court rejected an ACLU lawsuit challenging limits on the amount of funds a candidate could accept from sources outside of Alaska. It found that "nonresident contributions may be individually modest, but can cumulatively overwhelm Alaskans' political contributions. Without restraints, Alaska's elected officials can be subject to purchased or coerced influence which is grossly disproportionate to the support nonresidents' views have among the Alaska electorate."[110]

Albuquerque's Defiance

Rather than repealing its voter-enacted spending limits after the *Buckley* ruling, Albuquerque, New Mexico, just left them on the books. By the late 1990s, the limits had been indexed to $79,476 for mayor and $7,947 for city council, and they were working well.

Since 1974, when the limits were enacted, the city had seen an average voter turnout in local elections of 44 percent, while other cities in the region typically saw turnout rates of 10 to 12 percent.[111] Rather than protecting incumbents, as some argue, the limits had benefited challengers. In fact, incumbent mayors were defeated four times under the limits.

Mayoral candidate Joe Diaz wanted to spend more than the limit—he wanted to have more speech than anyone else. The chance to say whatever he wanted in more than fifty free community candidate forums wasn't enough; he wanted to use paid speech to force-feed his message to those who didn't want to hear it. So, Diaz went to court. A judge suspended the law and Diaz spent all he wanted to. He lost anyway and then dropped his lawsuit, which allowed the limits to go back into effect.

In 2001, Rick Homans again challenged the limits as part of his campaign for mayor. A lower court again suspended the law and this time the ruling was upheld by an appeals court, leaving them unenforced. Albuquerque appealed to the US Supreme Court.

Unlike the federal post-Watergate law, which the Supreme Court considered on an expedited, fact-free basis, Albuquerque provided a track record for the Court to consider. Judges didn't need to guess what appeared to be corrupt; there were surveys demonstrating what voters thought was corrupt. They didn't need to guess whether the limits would harm challengers or make it impossible to campaign for office; Albuquerque's experience proved otherwise. But the Supreme Court wasn't interested in evidence. It refused to hear Albuquerque's appeal, allowing the lower court ruling to stand.

In 1998, a federal appeals court struck down Cincinnati's spending limits in city council elections. Unlike Albuquerque's law, which had been on the books for decades, Cincinnati passed its law in 1995 in open defiance of the Supreme Court. The National Voting Rights Institute took up Cincinnati's case.

The Center for Responsive Politics conducted a study, which found that "the rise in the overall cost of city council races has caused a corresponding rise in the influence of wealthy donors in the City's elections, with such donors increasingly dominating the campaign financing process . . . and small donors . . . becoming marginal players in that process."[112]

An opinion survey agreed, finding that most city residents felt large contributions wielded undue influence, that ordinary voters could not participate politically on equal footing, that big money candidates drowned out other candidates, and that money undermined the fairness and integrity of the political system. The lower court said that none of these problems amounted to bribery, so under *Buckley's* precedent the spending limits had to go.

The two judges who signed the Cincinnati opinion actually believed that the Supreme Court was wrong in *Buckley* and that "the government has an important interest in leveling the electoral playing field by constraining the cost of federal campaigns."[113] The opinion agreed with Supreme Court justice Byron White's dissent in *Buckley*, which said, "It is quite wrong to assume that the net effect of limits on contributions and expenditures—which tend to protect equal access to the political arena, to free candidates and their staffs from the interminable burden of fund-raising, and to diminish the importance of repetitive 30-second commercials—will be adverse to the interest on informed debate protected by the First Amendment." But these judges didn't think they should uphold the Constitution as *they* read it. Like most federal judges, they felt their job was to uphold the US Supreme Court's precedent in *Buckley*, even if it was wrong.

A Brief Moment of Hope

For a while, it looked like the 2000s would be different than the 1990s.

On January 24, 2000, the US Supreme Court reinstated Missouri's contribution limits in the case *Nixon v. Shrink Missouri Government PAC*. These were no longer the $100 limits approved by voters, but rather $250 limits that the legislature had put in place in an attempt to head off the citizens' initiative. The Court ruled, correctly, that a state may adopt whatever contribution limits it sees fit so long as they are not "so radical in effect as to render political association ineffective, drive the sound of a candidate's voice below the level of notice, and render contributions pointless." Had the Court continued to use this commonsense standard to evaluate limits on paid speech, the political landscape over the last few decades might have been quite different.

Based upon the Missouri ruling, lower courts upheld contribution limits of $100 per election in Montana and $200 per election cycle in Vermont. The Montana court noted that two witnesses

> testified that they had to work harder and talk to more
> people in order to raise the same amount of campaign
> money. While this may be true, it is precisely the pur-
> pose behind contribution limitations; for candidates to
> acquire a broad and diverse base of support to eliminate
> undue influence, or the appearance thereof, from large
> contributors.[114]

The Vermont court found that "contribution limits may in point of fact actually improve candidate-voter communication by lessening the need for candidates to concentrate on wooing big donors. By diminishing the need for targeted pandering, these limits arguably enhance, rather than limit, a candidate's freedom to communicate."[115]

Then, in 2003, the Supreme Court upheld most of the federal Bipartisan Campaign Reform Act (a.k.a. McCain-Feingold) by a vote of five to four. In upholding a ban on using corporate and union treasury funds even in independent

campaigns, the Court went beyond *Buckley's* narrow definition of corruption.

The Court recognized what Justice Souter noted in the
Missouri ruling as "the cynical assumption that large donors
call the tune could jeopardize the willingness of voters to
take part in democratic governance."[116] The Court also relied
on a previous opinion, *Austin v. Michigan Chamber of Commerce*, which noted the "corrosive and distorting effects of
immense aggregations of wealth that are accumulated with
the help of the corporate form and that have little or no correlation to the public's support for the corporation's political
ideas."[117] When large donors call the tune or distort the
debate, they don't necessarily bribe anyone; they just have
unequal influence—something the *Buckley* court refused to
acknowledge.

Good-Bye Frying Pan; Hello Fire

By 2006, the court flip-flopped again for the worse. President George W. Bush replaced retiring justices Sandra Day
O'Connor and William Rehnquist, both conservatives who
had upheld limits on big money in politics, with Samuel
Alito and John Roberts. All four were appointed by Republican presidents, but Alito and Roberts proved to be much
more in sync with big money and corporations than their
predecessors. Although our Founders never intended it,
changing personnel on our Supreme Court in effect now
changes our Constitution.

The Supreme Court took up Vermont's law and exam-
ined mandatory spending limits for the first time since 1976.
Not only did the court reject the spending limits, but it
reversed the course it set in Missouri and struck down Vermont's contribution limits as well.

In 2007, the Court again backtracked on its recent toler-
ance of campaign finance laws. In *FEC v. Wisconsin Right to
Life*, the new 5–4 majority on the Roberts Court said that a
nonprofit corporation could fund political attack ads so long
as they could be reasonably interpreted as anything besides
an effort to defeat that candidate. An ad telling viewers to
"call their senator" and tell her to stop supporting an unpopular issue could be construed as an effort to persuade the
senator on the issue, not un-elect her. This led to a renewed
explosion of the so-called "issue ad loophole" that 527 organizations (political advocacy groups) had begun to exploit in
the 1990s.

The Immaculate Conception of *Citizens United*

James Bopp, the lawyer who had brought the case from Wisconsin, then saw a strategic opening in David Bossie's cause.

While he was a congressional staffer, Bossie had uncov-
ered some unflattering history about Hillary and Bill Clinton. After House Speaker Newt Gingrich forced him to
resign over ethical lapses, Bossie became president of a nonprofit group calling itself Citizens United. Bossie promptly
filed a complaint at the Federal Elections Commission alleg-
ing that a Michael Moore film criticizing President Bush
violated new campaign finance laws. When that complaint
went nowhere, Bossie and Bopp figured they had found yet
another loophole in the law.[118]

Bossie produced a film called *Hillary: The Movie*,
which was critical of Senator Hillary Clinton, then running her first presidential campaign. The movie itself was
clearly part of the free press, not paid speech, by the simple fact that viewers sought out the opportunity to watch it
through a pay-for-view cable network. But Bossie wanted

to use unlimited funds not only to pay for thirty-second TV ads that both promoted the film and attacked Hillary Clinton but to subsidize the pay-for-view cable channel—paying it to abandon its normal marketplace practices and instead offer the movie for free. The ads alone violated the McCain-Feingold provision against using corporate funds to attack a candidate within sixty days of an election. Citizens United sued the Federal Election Commission, asking the courts to step in.

The Supreme Court could have done two fairly reasonable things. First, it could have told Bossie that he could use Citizens United's anonymous and unlimited donations from corporations and others to pay for production costs of the film because that was protected under freedom of the press. Second, the Court could have held that any funds to pay for the thirty-second TV ads and otherwise promote the film would need to come solely from individuals and be disclosed through a political committee. These two things were all Citizens United needed to produce and promote the film, and the case would have been insignificant.

John Roberts actually drafted a narrow ruling that would have done exactly these two things and no more.[119] Anthony Kennedy wrote a more radical opinion arguing that the Court should go further and invalidate the McCain-Feingold law. Roberts used Kennedy's opinion as an excuse to flip-flop, and he joined Kennedy's sweeping decision to gut most of the law.

More Highly Unusual Proceedings

Justice Souter then wrote a scathing dissent that accused Chief Justice Roberts of violating the Court's operating principles in order to manufacture an outcome that fit his personal ideology.[120] Courts, you see, are only supposed to rule on the case in front of them, not reach out and make policy above and beyond the issues in the case. Souter's dissent never became public, because Roberts struck a deal with him to do something courts almost never do.

Rather than ruling on the narrow issue in front of it, as judges are supposed to, the Supreme Court told David Bossie he hadn't asked for enough. Roberts ordered Citizens United to come back in the fall and argue that the Court should reverse its own recent precedent and allow unlimited corporate spending for any political attack ad, not just Bossie's movie.

To justify its 180-degree reversal from recent precedent, the Roberts Court brazenly invented its own version of reality. Five justices decided that "independent expenditures, including those made by corporations, do not give rise to corruption or the appearance of corruption."[121] Never mind that most Americans thought otherwise—these five men in black robes were going to decide for us what appeared corrupt and what didn't.

"To justify its 180-degree reversal from recent precedent, the Roberts Court brazenly invented its own version of reality."

They might just as well have declared that the sky shall not appear blue.

The decision to substitute the Court's own judgment of what is corrupting for the people's judgment was the same thing the Court had done in *Buckley*. Justice Byron White, in dissenting to *Buckley*, noted that corruption should have been a good enough reason to limit campaign spending and questioned the Court's decision to swap its own definition of corruption for Congress's definition:

> *Congress was plainly of the view that these expendi-*
> *tures also have corruptive potential, but the Court*
> *strikes down the provision, strangely enough, claiming*
> *more insight as to what may improperly influence can-*
> *didates than is possessed by the majority of Congress*
> *that passed this bill and the President who signed it.*[122]

The *Citizens United* court explicitly overruled not only its recent ruling upholding McCain-Feingold, but also the earlier *Austin v. Michigan Chamber of Commerce* ruling upholding a ban on using corporate treasury funds for political campaigns. *Citizens United* actually harkened way back to the 1886 case *Santa Clara County v. Southern Pacific Railroad.* In that ruling, the chief justice at the time claimed that corporations were entitled to Fourteenth Amendment protection as persons. (In fact, that case never actually said this, but that is beyond the scope of this book.)[123]

The Age of Super PACs

Contrary to popular belief, the *Citizens United* ruling did not create super PACs—the supposedly independent campaigns that collect unlimited checks on behalf of candidates—although its bizarre logic that it was impossible for independent spending to corrupt legislators did pave the way for their rise and impact.

Super PACs were born from a case known as *Speech-Now.org v. FEC,* which came a few months later. In this case, a lower court struck down the $5,000 limit on contributions to political action committees (PACs) that had been established by Congress in the 1974 post-Watergate law. This meant that any PAC that didn't make direct donations to candidates no longer faced contribution limits—they became super PACs. Presidential candidates in the 2012 election began having their allies and family members set up super PACs to receive massive checks and spend them to benefit a single candidate—effectively gutting the candidate contribution limits. There was no longer even half a baby left of the post-Watergate law.

When Fairness Became Unconstitutional

The Roberts Five weren't done.

Although the *Buckley* opinion held we couldn't limit campaign spending in order to promote political equality, it did allow public financing to level the playing field. The Roberts Court would have none of it. It struck down an Arizona law that gave public funds to a candidate being outspent by big money interests so he or she could respond.

What is interesting about this ruling is that the Court majority admitted that one candidate's speech is diminished when other people spend money against him. The Roberts Court held that a well-funded candidate was harmed when his opponent received additional public funds, even though it didn't change the amount the first candidate spent. So, when it suits their personal ideologies, the Roberts Five are just fine with limiting some voices in order to enhance others, just so long as those spending levels aren't fair or equal.

"This Court," wrote Justice Roberts, "has repeatedly rejected the argument that the government has a compelling state interest in 'leveling the playing field.'"[124] John Roberts would have us believe that self-government *requires* political inequality.

Fat Cats *Still* Weren't Satisfied

Spending unlimited and ungodly amounts independently to elect as many candidates as he wanted wasn't enough for Alabama energy mogul Shaun McCutcheon. McCutcheon wanted to give checks directly to candidates so their ads could speak for him (and perhaps so the candidates would listen to him when they called on the phone asking for his money).

As rich man James Buckley had done before him, rich man Shaun McCutcheon went to the Supreme Court, which cheerfully obliged. In *McCutcheon v. FEC*, the Court eviscerated limits on how much one rich person could give all candidates combined. Those limits, set by Congress in 1974, had risen to $123,200 as of 2013, so they only actually limited a few hundred extremely wealthy people—Shaun McCutcheon among them.

Justice Roberts, in writing the opinion, again conflated paid speech with the free press, saying "the government may no more restrict how many candidates or causes a donor may support than it may tell a newspaper how many candidates it may endorse."[125]

During the oral arguments, Justice Scalia quipped that since the Court had already established in *Citizens United* that it was not possibly corrupting for a wealthy donor to buy influence and gratitude with independent expenditures, the Court must allow Mr. McCutcheon to buy as much influence with as many politicians as he wanted.

Ironically, in cases involving elected judges raising campaign contributions or benefiting from massive independent expenditure campaigns, John Roberts has acknowledged that big money can unduly sway elected officials. Roberts thinks that it is perfectly fine for legislators to be "responsive" to big money donors but not for judges, who need to "observe the utmost fairness."[126]

Who's in Charge?—The Proper Role for the Courts in a Republic

At this point, you may be wondering when the American people granted authority to five members of the Supreme Court to decide for us what *we* think is corrupting and what isn't. After all, if the legitimacy of a republic depends on the consent of the governed, surely we must have consented to this somewhere along the way.

We did not.

Our Constitution does not grant the Supreme Court the authority to substitute its own judgment for the judgment of the people. The Constitution never even granted the Supreme Court authority to declare laws unconstitutional.

The Court simply took that power.

We let them do it without much protest, but silence does not equal consent.

The Constitution says that judicial power includes the authority to consider all cases "arising under this Constitution" as well as the laws of the United States. But the Framers of our Constitution did not agree on whether this included the power to declare a law unconstitutional. Rather, most of the Founders expected the separation of powers between the state and federal governments as well as between the three branches of government to preserve the ability of the people to act as the final arbiters of our Constitution.[127]

Things began to change in the decades following adoption of the Constitution. In the famous case *Marbury v.*

Madison of 1803, the US Supreme Court declared an act of Congress to be unconstitutional and a majority of people in the country then accepted this as a proper role for the Court.

But just because the Court issued a judgment didn't mean that the Court was the *only* institution involved in interpreting our Constitution. As the former Stanford Law School dean Larry Kramer has noted, "Judges were no more authoritative on these matters than any other public official, and their judgments about the meaning of the Constitution, like those of everyone else, were still subject to oversight and ultimate resolution by the people themselves."[128]

People did not take up arms after the Supreme Court began issuing opinions as to whether laws were constitutional, so arguably we consented to this role. But later in our history, we did in fact take up arms in opposition to the Supreme Court's pro-slavery ruling in *Dred Scott*. In his first inaugural address, President Abraham Lincoln noted:

> *I do not forget the position assumed by some that constitutional questions are to be decided by the Supreme Court. . . . But, if the policy of the government, upon vital questions, affecting the whole people, is to be irrevocably fixed by decisions of the Supreme Court, the instant they are made . . . the people will have ceased to be their own rulers.*[129]

Some legal scholars have suggested that we take a step back and abolish judicial review of the constitutionality of our laws altogether.[130] Whether that is a bad or good idea is beyond this book's purpose. Regardless, we need not go that far in order to reverse the logic of unlimited campaign money as free speech, as embodied in *Buckley v. Valeo* and subsequent rulings.

We simply need to remember that Supreme Court opinions are just that—*opinions*. State courts, legislators, attorneys general, and presidents should take those Supreme Court opinions into account when they exercise their own duty to uphold and defend our Constitution and our laws. But they should not abdicate the responsibility to come to their own conclusions or to consider and honor the conclusions of the American people.

Likewise, citizens should take Supreme Court opinions into account when we make ultimate decisions about how we govern ourselves, but those decisions in the end remain up to us. The next chapters will explore various ways we Americans can reclaim our sovereignty to decide for ourselves how money shall be spent on political advertising and campaigns.

What you can do: Stamp it out

Use a rubber stamp to put a message demanding an end to *Citizens United* on your dollar bills and literally let your money speak. Check out www.stamp stampede.org for details and to order your stamp.

PART 2 | READY FOR ACTION? LET'S GO

Chapter 5

Repairing Our Republic

How the People Can Overturn the Court

*[Chief Justice] John Marshall has made his
decision, now let him enforce it.*

—President Andrew Jackson

Unelected judges have trampled our right to determine what
corrupts and how we want to govern ourselves. They tell us
we cannot give every voice equal time in public debate but
that we are required to let a few billionaires drown out the
rest of us. This issue goes beyond campaign contributions
and spending; it is a question of sovereignty. Will we allow
ourselves to be conquered from within by an elite group of
billionaires and their judicial accomplices?

If not, what can we do?

This chapter will explore several ways to overturn a
wrongheaded court ruling. Although all approaches have
merit, organizing support for a constitutional amendment is
our best opportunity, with the most permanent effect, to
really get big money out of politics once and for all. The
amendment fight could also build a citizens movement capa-
ble of winning a whole range of reforms to restore representative democracy to the United States. For example, the
effort around the Equal Rights Amendment succeeded in

building a movement that won more equal pay for women, more women in elected office (although still not enough), and women serving in the military even while failing (so far) to change the text in our Constitution.

But before settling on an amendment as one central approach, let's examine all our options.

We Could Try to Change Their Minds

Like everyone, Supreme Court justices sometimes make mistakes. Sometimes they fix them. In fact, more than two hundred opinions of the Supreme Court have reversed previous rulings.[131]

It takes some intellectual courage to admit you were wrong. Chief Justice Roberts changed his mind about whether to issue a narrow or sweeping ruling in the *Citizens United* case. He could, theoretically, change it back.

In a 1992 case about abortion, Justice Kennedy initially wanted to overturn *Roe v. Wade*. However, while drafting the opinion, Kennedy changed his mind partly because he felt the Court would lose credibility if it didn't respect its past opinions.

Kennedy's flip-flop switched the vote from 5–4 to overturn *Roe* to 5–4 to sustain it. His concern about institutional credibility is a reminder that advocating for the Supreme Court to reverse itself may not be the best strategy for those who care about its reputation and who otherwise advocate for upholding precedent. Notably, Kennedy's example and Justice Roberts' change in *Citizens United* came prior to issuing the Court's final opinion, suggesting that justices have some space to go back and forth until they declare a public position by joining an opinion or dissent. Once that occurs, it's harder to switch.

Rare as it may be for justices to change their public positions, it happens. In 1968, Chief Justice Earl Warren voted for the *Bruton v. United States* ruling, overturning a previous ruling (*Delli Paoli v. United States*) he had supported in 1957.

But the fact is, Supreme Court members rarely even have the opportunity to reverse themselves. To change a precedent, the Court must consider a similar case and come to a different conclusion. Because legislators have limited time, they are reluctant to pass laws that are likely to be voided by the courts. Some legislators mistakenly believe it is improper to pass a law defying the Supreme Court—even if the legislator thinks the law is constitutional. It usually takes decades before an opportunity to reverse a past ruling presents itself to the Court. By then, the judges who issued the original opinion are gone.

Rather than forcing a member of the Supreme Court to admit he was wrong, reformers may have more luck presenting arguments that the Court hasn't considered. This is why academics and lawyers put so much energy into inventing other "compelling" reasons for the Court to limit money in politics besides the reasons it has agreed to (a narrow form of corruption) and rejected (equality.) Although the new reasons (e.g., integrity of the electoral process) look and sound a lot like the old reasons repackaged in new bottles, they provide plausible rationale for a judge to issue a different ruling while saving face. It's useful to give a judge a way out of an untenable spot, but saving face only becomes necessary if public distrust first weakens the moral authority of the court.

We Could Wait for New Justices— and Cross Our Fingers

As the *Citizens United* ruling demonstrated, when members of the Court are replaced by new members, it can change the vote count and in effect change our Constitution.

In *Brown v. Board of Education*, the Supreme Court reversed a previous opinion upholding racially separate but equal education. None of the justices who heard the original case in 1896 were even alive when the Court reversed itself in 1954.

The *Brown* opinion was surely the wise choice for our country, and it is often held up as a positive accomplishment of an "activist" court. Note, however, that while *Brown* did overrule state legislative and executive officials, the Court acted in response to a populist civil rights movement that could honestly claim to represent the majority will of the American people.

The Court also had the full support of the federal executive branch, which sent in federal troops to enforce the act. Congress, too, ratified the Court's stance by passing major civil rights legislation in the 1960s. Moreover, the Court acted unanimously.

A 9–0 ruling that reverses distant precedent with the support of most Americans and all three branches of the federal government is substantially different, and more legitimate, than a 5–4 ruling reversing recent precedent and defying the clearly expressed will of the people, the Congress, and the president.

Voters have little direct involvement in this process of constitutional change through court turnover. Some citizens decide their votes for president partially on how a new president could impact the Court, but this is hardly foolproof.

Justices John Paul Stevens and David Souter, appointed by Republican presidents Ford and George Bush Sr., were more liberal than many Republican voters wished. Likewise, some of the names on the short list of potential nominees reportedly considered by President Obama have written articles supporting the *Citizens United* and *Buckley* rulings.[132]

Waiting for a new lineup of justices feels a bit like rolling the dice with our Constitution. There's a somewhat twisted game called ghoul pools or death pools where participants enter the names of famous people they predict will die in the coming year. At year's end, whoever has the most correct guesses wins. In the same vein, Supreme Court watchers now guess which justice will retire, or die, during any president's term. The meaning of our foundational document could change depending upon who has a heart attack—not exactly a thoughtful way to govern ourselves.

As the Supreme Court increasingly makes controversial policy decisions by 5–4 votes, confirmation battles in the Senate have become politicized. Each confirmation of a new justice becomes a vote on numerous and unspecified changes to our Constitution that will last a generation, if not longer. Senators try in vain to ascertain what a nominee really thinks so that they can understand what changes to the Constitution might arise from putting him or her on the Court. Judicial nominees duck specific answers, taking the power to change our Constitution and make policy out of the hands of elected senators and leaving it in the hands of judges with lifetime appointments but often little real-life experience.

Constitutional changes arising from new court personnel lack the authority of a formal amendment to the Constitution. Although they can have enormous impacts on any one generation of Americans, the changes are not as permanent.

If the current 5–4 composition of the Supreme Court changed overnight so that there was a 5–4 majority of members favoring limits on money in politics, we might have ten or twenty years of sane policy in this arena. But then, the majority could tilt back in the other direction just as suddenly.

Having our fundamental rules about self-government flip back and forth every few decades based upon the whimsy of whoever happens to sit on the Supreme Court is not a way to take our Constitution, or self-government, seriously. Americans should seek opportunities to encourage the Supreme Court to correct its own errors regarding money in politics, but we should cement those rulings through a formal amendment even if the Court temporarily comes to its senses.

We Could Pass a Constitutional Amendment

If "We the People" believe that a majority of Supreme Court members are misreading the Constitution, we can make the Constitution more explicit.

"Organizing support for a constitutional amendment is our best opportunity, with the most permanent effect, to really get big money out of politics once and for all."

Although difficult to achieve, a constitutional amendment offers the most durable solution because it elicits the greatest chance for public engagement. Three-quarters of the states (currently thirty-eight) are needed to pass an amendment. But each state must approve the exact same words, so who drafts the proposal?

Article V of the Constitution provides for two methods of drafting. Two-thirds of both houses in Congress can propose the amendment through drafting, debating, and passing a joint resolution. This was the method used for all twenty-seven of the amendments enacted so far. State legislatures could also call a special convention of state delegates to draft an amendment, a method I'll discuss in chapter 8.

Some lawyers—who by nature and training tend to elevate the importance of courts and judges relative to the importance of voters and legislators—profess that it is simply "too hard" to pass a constitutional amendment. It is indeed time-consuming, but so is waiting decades for the composition of the Court to change and then bringing a new case to the court.

What elites often mean when they say that the amendment process is "too hard" is that they would prefer to have well-educated lawyers and judges handle this rather than reminding ordinary people that we have the authority to overturn the Supreme Court.[133] Both liberal and conservative elites wish to maintain the perceived "supremacy" of the Supreme Court in running the country in ways they find superior to what ordinary people can achieve. As one observer put it:

> *I suspect that some people think that a campaign finance amendment is a bad idea because they think the Supreme Court should be asked to overrule Buckley v. Valeo. There is nothing wrong with asking the Court to do what you want . . . [but] it strikes me as a bit peculiar to prefer doing that to finding out directly what the people want by seeking to amend the*

Constitution. Or, if not peculiar, at least rather openly antidemocratic.[134]

Former senator Russ Feingold, for instance, vehemently denounces the *Citizens United* ruling, which gutted the law bearing his name. Yet Feingold cannot bring himself to support a constitutional amendment to overturn it and in fact openly opposed such an amendment when he was in the Senate. At the end of the day, many elites don't trust us to govern ourselves.

We Can Pick a Fight That Spurs a Constitutional Crisis

All people have a fundamental right to alter or abolish their government anytime they want. Our current Constitution provides a peaceful way to alter it through a formal amendment process as described in Article V.

But that doesn't mean that an Article V process is the only way.

Sometimes, Americans have found creative ways to pick a fight with the status quo and win it so decisively that our foundational agreement about government changes.

Our current Constitution was born out of a crisis of our previous foundational agreement, the Articles of Confederation. The articles stated that they only could be amended by unanimous approval of all thirteen states, but our current Constitution didn't follow that prescribed process—it only required ratification by nine of the thirteen. Nonetheless, even the opponents of the new Constitution had to concede that the people had spoken through a legitimate process, albeit one other than what the Articles of Confederation prescribed, and the new Constitution was deemed legitimate.[135]

Some scholars have argued that we in effect amend our Constitution in a more permanent and legitimate fashion when these changes come about as a result of a constitutional crisis rather than through simple court reversal. In the crisis, different branches of government adopt opposing views, which the voters then choose between in a national election.[136] The national election becomes a way for the people to speak directly and resolve the crisis when one branch backs down in the face of overwhelming public support for the other branch.

Perhaps the best example of a constitutional crisis that changed constitutional understanding was Franklin Delano Roosevelt pushing the Supreme Court to a crisis over disagreements about the constitutionality of the New Deal.

We Could Pack the Court

Courts of the early twentieth century were as hostile to government regulation of the economy as the Roberts Court is to regulating money in politics. Judges began striking down rules for a more just economy in 1905 with a case known as *Lochner v. New York*, where the Supreme Court voided a law limiting the workweek to sixty hours. The Supreme Court then rejected law after law protecting economic fairness, arguing that this was beyond the scope of the government and violated the private right to contract.

In 1924, Congress reacted to the *Lochner*-era Supreme Court rulings by proposing a very limited constitutional amendment to allow for restrictions of child labor. But, prior to the Great Depression, public support for the measure was not yet sufficiently strong. By 1927, twenty-six state legislatures rejected the amendment while only five had ratified it.[137]

When the Massachusetts legislature issued a ballot asking voters if it should approve the amendment, an overwhelming majority opposed the idea.[138]

After the stock market crash of 1929, a new era was born. Fourteen legislatures ratified the child labor amendment in 1933 and another eight did so by 1937. Still, it wasn't quite enough.

In 1935, the Supreme Court remained staunchly opposed to enforcing any rules in the marketplace. President Roosevelt had passed the National Industrial Recovery Act through Congress, a plan to rebuild the economy decimated by the Great Depression. The Supreme Court unanimously struck down the act just two months after it had been upheld by an appellate court. President Roosevelt declared the Court's action as "more important than any decision probably since the *Dred Scott* case."[139] Many of today's leaders are saying similar things about *Citizens United*.

President Roosevelt considered several responses to the Court, including a formal constitutional amendment to authorize the New Deal. Members of Congress had already proposed thirty-nine amendments along those lines.[140] One idea to speed up the process was for an amendment to be ratified by state conventions, instead of state legislatures, that would all meet on a presidentially selected day. The special elections to select those convention members would serve as a national referendum on the New Deal amendment.

The president also considered a proposal by Senator Burton Wheeler to pass a constitutional amendment that would severely limit judicial review of laws. Senator Wheeler's idea was that Congress could reenact any law voided by the Court and have it automatically be constitutional so long as the people had a chance to weigh in on the matter through an intervening congressional election. Had Roosevelt chosen this path, Congress could have reversed the *Buckley v. Valeo* decision in 1977 simply by reenacting the post-Watergate reforms.

However, Roosevelt felt that a formal amendment process would take too long to address the severe economic crisis that threatened the very stability and existence of the United States. That crisis led him to a more immediate plan. He would "pack" the Supreme Court by appointing additional justices who would uphold the New Deal. There was nothing illegal about the plan. An 1869 act of Congress had established the nine-justice level and Roosevelt correctly noted that Congress could change that number.

Some members of Roosevelt's own party thought the court-packing plan was unseemly even if not illegal. Many were hesitant to support it.

But the Court blinked first.

Three weeks after Roosevelt introduced his legislation to increase the size of the Court, the Court switched its position on economic regulation, upholding a minimum wage law by a 5–4 ruling. In particular, Justice Owen Roberts (no relation to John Roberts) switched his vote from his previous opinions. Roberts' sudden flip-flop has become known as the "switch in time that saved nine," meaning the Court had backed away from the constitutional crisis by upholding the New Deal and in so doing preserved a nine-member court. Roosevelt lost the battle to pack the court but won the war to save the New Deal and restore the US economy.

It's possible to view Owen Roberts' flip-flop purely as a move by a self-interested institution to preserve its own power and reputation. The Court had just been repudiated by a national election that overwhelmingly elected candidates who campaigned against the Court's rulings. But courts ever since have continued to uphold government rules to ensure fairness in the marketplace.

The Supreme Court's "switch in time" was the moment when it recognized that the People had indeed spoken about this issue, in effect changing our Constitution. The People had not done this through a formal amendment to the Constitution but rather by speaking clearly through their votes to back the president during a constitutional crisis where he challenged the Court.

We Could Throw the Bums Out

Even without changing the number of justices, Congress could change the composition of the Court by removing a justice through impeachment. Congress has forced out a Supreme Court member before—Abe Fortas resigned in 1969 in order to prevent being impeached. Fortas had received $15,000 in speaking fees from American University—funds that originally came from private sources that may have had business before the Supreme Court. He also accepted $20,000 from a family foundation.

Abe Fortas's ethical lapses pale in comparison to the ethical transgressions of current justice Clarence Thomas. For more than a decade, Thomas lied on federal forms that he signed under oath. Thomas said his wife, Ginni, had received no outside income when in fact she had received more than $700,000 from the Heritage Foundation. Ginni Thomas also benefitted financially from the *Citizens United* ruling because an organization she ran was allowed to accept unlimited corporate donations as a result, yet Justice Thomas did not recuse himself from that case.

In addition, Thomas appears to have accepted gifts and luxury travel from the Dallas developer Harlan Crow while aiding Crow in a charitable fund-raising project, which he failed to report.

In January 2008, the same month Citizens United released its movie critical of Hillary Clinton, Thomas appeared at secret political strategy sessions held by billionaires Charles and David Koch as well as at fund-raisers for the Federalist Society. These actions violate the judicial code of conduct, which means they would be grounds for removal for any federal judge—but not Supreme Court members, who do not feel bound by that code. Some members of Congress have reacted by introducing legislation that would require the Supreme Court to adhere to a code of ethics, but Congress has not passed the bill. Nor has the House moved to impeach Thomas.

Setting aside ethical problems, there is the more difficult question of whether a Supreme Court member could be removed simply because a majority of the House and two-thirds of the Senate strongly disagree with his or her interpretation of the Constitution.

The House of Representatives impeached Justice Samuel Chase in 1804, in large part for using the bench to advance his partisan political views. The Senate acquitted Chase because senators of both parties worried that removing a judge for partisan behavior would compromise the independence of the judiciary. But surely there must be some point where Congress might conclude that a member of the Court was no longer exhibiting good behavior—the constitutional standard for impeachment—based on their judicial actions.

Suppose that a single justice wrote a dissenting opinion that grossly misinterpreted constitutional principles, such as calling for the return of poll taxes. What would Congress do? Or suppose a judge rejected laws against bank robbery on the absurd grounds that money is speech and thieves are only helping the bank customers disseminate their political views? Would that be grounds for impeachment? What if five justices ruled a bank manager could take his customers' money and spend it on things the customers didn't authorize? How about a corporate CEO who used his shareholders' money for political spending that the shareholders didn't authorize? Some would say that the *Citizens United* ruling has allowed CEOs to do precisely that.

Have the Roberts Five crossed the line?

Some people think so and are ready to impeach the justices who signed the *Citizens United* opinion.[141] Most Americans, however, are still uncomfortable impeaching judges purely for their ideology, even if it's reactionary. But if a judge flatly ignored any new amendment to the Constitution, thereby violating the oath of office to support and defend the Constitution, that would likely be viewed as grounds for impeachment.

Political Disobedience: Congress and the President Could Defy the Court

Through civil disobedience, Americans have occasionally broken the law in order to protest a fundamental injustice. During the civil rights movement, black Americans were arrested for eating at white-only lunch counters, for instance. Suppose entire branches of government took this approach?

If a majority of voters demand it, the legislative and executive branches could pass and enforce a law to limit big money in political campaigns over the objections of the Supreme Court. Indeed, while campaigning for president in 2012, Newt Gingrich said that if elected he would ignore Supreme Court rulings he disagreed with in some circumstances.[142]

Several 2016 Republican presidential candidates vowed similar defiance of the Supreme Court's ruling on gay marriage, although they were also defying a majority of Americans with this position.

Judges must sentence those who violate our laws, and this is where a defiance strategy would play out. A lower court would need to sentence a person convicted of violating any campaign spending limit, providing an opportunity to test the US Supreme Court by sending a new case up for appeal. If the Court found the law unconstitutional and the executive branch punished violators anyhow, some members of Congress would try to impeach the president for defying the Court and the battle lines would be drawn. That impeachment process would present a constitutional crisis that allowed the people to speak on the matter. If the president withstood impeachment, the Court would be repudiated.

I am not suggesting that individuals should be free to disobey any law they disagree with. Rather, our Framers intended all three branches of government to act according to their own independent judgment of both the law and the Constitution, even if it means defying other branches. When backed by a majority of Americans, institutional defiance is not an assault on the rule of law, it is an attempt to abide by the law. The only question is who should make the law, judges or legislators.

Others have suggested that Congress could neuter the Court with the exceptions clause, Article III, Section 2 of the Constitution, which says that "the Supreme Court shall have appellate jurisdiction . . . with such exceptions, and under such regulations as the Congress shall make." Congress could pass a law limiting money in politics with a provision excluding Supreme Court jurisdiction to review it.[143] Former congressman Ron Paul had actually introduced legislation to strip federal courts of jurisdiction in other core First Amendment areas.[144] Remember that judicial review is not stipulated in the Constitution. Rather it was a practice later asserted by the courts, which has since become widely accepted.

States Could Defy Federal Courts

Several states have recently defied federal law by legalizing marijuana for medical or recreational use. These states have put the president in the position of choosing to enforce the federal ban on marijuana sales or back down and defer to the states. States could take a similar approach to money in politics.

At first glance, states have a strong argument for passing laws limiting campaign spending in open defiance of federal courts. The First Amendment makes no mention of the states, saying only that "*Congress* shall make no law respecting an establishment of religion, or prohibiting the free exercise thereof; or abridging the freedom of speech, or of the press . . ." (emphasis added)

When Congress passed the Sedition Act in 1798, which clearly violated the First Amendment by prohibiting speech that defamed the president, Thomas Jefferson and others who opposed the law did not go to the Supreme Court. First of all, that Court was appointed by federalists who supported all four of the Alien and Sedition Acts. Furthermore, the idea that the Supreme Court could declare laws unconstitutional was not yet established. Instead, Jefferson took to the states. He drafted resolutions for the Kentucky and Virginia legislatures that declared the federal law unconstitutional, null, and void.

Jefferson's Kentucky resolution specifically spoke to the question of state versus federal role in determining free speech rules:

> *The powers not delegated to the United States by the Constitution, nor prohibited by it to the States, are reserved to the States respectively, or to the people; and that no power over the freedom of religion, freedom of speech, or freedom of the press being delegated to the United States by the Constitution, nor prohibited by it to the States, all lawful powers respecting the same did of right remain, and were reserved to the States or the people; that thus was manifested their determination to retain to themselves the right of judging how far the licentiousness of speech and of the press may be abridged without lessening their useful freedom.*[145]

Jefferson clearly thought *states* could abridge free speech. He explicitly said so years later in a letter to Abigail Adams: "While we deny that Congress have a right to control the freedom of the press, we have ever asserted the right of the States, and their exclusive right, to do so."[146]

Although there is no reason to believe that Jefferson or other Founders believed money was speech, even if they had, the Kentucky resolution makes clear that the states could actually limit speech, and therefore certainly limit campaign spending, even if the federal government could not.

Perhaps Jefferson was wrong in his contention that the states could abridge political speech. Article IV of the Constitution guarantees a "republican form of government." Federal courts could use that guarantee to insist on freedom of speech and press within the states in order to allow people to govern themselves.[147]

Moreover, most legal scholars believe that even if the First Amendment did not apply to states at the time of our founding, it did after the Civil War. The passage of the Fourteenth Amendment, which guaranteed equal protection to everyone (including former slaves), "incorporated" many federal rights to every state and explicitly restricted state power. However, there is not a legal consensus on exactly how far such incorporation goes. To the extent that the Fourteenth Amendment does incorporate the First Amendment, it elevates political equality as a reason to do so. State limits on campaign spending that advance a republican form of government and political equality are consistent with every word in our Constitution.

In contrast, the highly imaginative Roberts Court interpretation of the Constitution forbidding state limits on campaign spending goes something like this: 1) Our constitutional Framers thought unlimited campaign spending was free speech when they passed the First Amendment *and* 2) the Congress that drafted the Fourteenth Amendment to protect former slaves meant to force that bizarre "money as speech" interpretation upon state governments in order to protect the rights of rich plantation owners to unduly influence elections.

Really?

At the very least, given that federal judges do not agree among themselves on whether political advertising is free speech, you might think that self-proclaimed "judicially modest" federal judges would defer to state judges, state legislators, and even more so to the people acting directly through ballot initiatives and allow states to limit campaign money.

You would be wrong.

Montana Takes a Stand

In 1912, the people of Montana passed a voter initiative to ban corporate treasury funds from bankrolling state candidate campaigns. This law worked well until 2012.

Even after the *Citizens United* ruling, Steve Bullock, the Montana attorney general at the time, concluded he had a duty to uphold Montana's law consistent with how he viewed both the Montana and US constitutions. Bullock enforced the law, in brazen defiance of the US Supreme Court.

The big money group American Tradition Partnership sued. The case went up to the Montana Supreme Court, which upheld the state law in no uncertain terms by a vote of 7–2. Even the two dissenting judges agreed that the Montana law was constitutional but thought that a state court should not defy the US Supreme Court by acting contrary to the *Citizens United* ruling.

In its opinion, the Montana Supreme Court listed considerable evidence going back a hundred years about how corporate money had corrupted Montana politics.

But the US Supreme Court wasn't interested in evidence. It reversed the Montana Supreme Court without even holding a hearing. The Roberts Court had decided that corporate money could not ever be corrupting, period.

All evidence be damned.

At this point, Attorney General Bullock folded his tent and stopped enforcing the law.

But, suppose he hadn't? What happens when a state executive branch defies the federal judiciary? A constitutional crisis, that's what.

Former slave states thumbed their nose at the Fourteenth Amendment and any federal attempt to enforce equal rights for African Americans for nearly a century after federal troops withdrew from the South in 1877. The states made a mockery of our Constitution. It took nearly eighty years of Jim Crow discrimination before the federal government would attempt to enforce the Fourteenth Amendment.

After the *Brown v. Board of Education* Supreme Court ruling of 1954 to desegregate schools, the governor of Arkansas openly defied the Court. Against the wishes of the superintendent of schools and mayor of Little Rock, Governor Orval Faubus sent the Arkansas National Guard to physically block black students from attending a white school in Little Rock. President Dwight Eisenhower sent in federal troops, which took over the Arkansas National Guard. The federal executive branch enforced the federal court's order to resolve the constitutional crisis.

Now, suppose the president, the local citizens, the Congress, the state governor, the state legislature, and even the state and federal troops *all* agreed that a state attorney general who was enforcing a commonsense limit on corporations buying elections was upholding the Constitution.

Would President Obama really have sent in federal troops to prevent the Montana attorney general from enforcing a popular Montana law that had worked well for a hundred years? We will never know, as neither Steve Bullock nor Barack Obama chose to risk his political career forcing such a constitutional crisis.

But that doesn't mean some state or federal official won't in the future. What commander in chief will enforce a Court doctrine that campaign spending is free speech when the vast majority of Americans believe otherwise? If racists can ignore the Supreme Court and federal rights for nearly a century after Reconstruction, what is to prevent others with more virtuous intent? It turns out, it's happened—more than 150 years ago in Wisconsin.

In 1854, the Wisconsin Supreme Court refused to convict Sherman Booth, a newspaper editor who had encouraged a crowd to free an escaped slave from jail. Federal marshals had captured the slave, Joshua Glover, under the federal Fugitive Slave Act. The Wisconsin court not only released Booth, it declared the federal law unconstitutional.[148] To this day, the Wisconsin Supreme Court has refused to recognize the US Supreme Court's ruling upholding that law. Booth, meanwhile, was pardoned by President James Buchanan after federal courts convicted him. That's what can happen if you defy the Supreme Court but abide by the will of the people and the true spirit of our Constitution.

Work-Arounds

When computer programmers encounter a bug that has corrupted a program, they often devise what's called a work-around to make the program function even without fixing the actual bug or virus. Similarly, we could pass policies that will help reduce the effects of *Citizens United* and *Buckley v. Valeo*. For most of the 1980s and 1990s, this was how reformers proceeded—occasionally with some success.

State and federal laws have improved disclosure of money given to candidates and parties, although some of the big money then found dark places to hide in so-called 527 groups and other nonprofits.

Several states, notably Maine, Arizona, and Connecticut, have passed laws to provide public funds to candidates who demonstrate grassroots support. New York, Los Angeles, and other major cities have boosted the role of small donors by providing significant matching funds from public sources to candidates who accept limits on their contributions and spending. This has allowed candidates who do not cater to wealthy interests to run for office, and sometimes to win, even in the face of big money opposition.

An updated version of these laws, called anticorruption acts much like those a century ago, are now in circulation at the state and local level. Cities like Tallahassee have passed measures combining modest amounts of public financing with ethics measures. Harvard professor Lawrence Lessig launched a campaign for president around such a proposal.

Congress could require broadcasters that use the federal airwaves—which are public property—to make time available for free to candidates or political parties. Free airtime has been introduced in Congress for decades, only to be crushed by the broadcaster lobby. TV and radio stations, you see, make a tidy profit off all the political ads they sell.

Even if we can't yet beat the broadcasters, state and local election officials could publish digital voters' guides that provide every candidate for office the opportunity to make online videos available for voters to stream on their smartphone or computer whenever they wanted. These voters' guides would provide a level playing field, with each candidate getting the same number of videos, limited to the same amount of time. These guides could also link to debate footage, lists of endorsements, the candidates' own websites, and detailed data on campaign contributors supporting the candidate. It could be a one-stop shop for voters seeking information that would be superior to the paid speech we are getting in thirty-second attack ads on TV.

These work-arounds are important reforms that we should implement even if we are able to establish limits on big money in politics. Even with such limits in place, there will still be people's voices we need to hear.

Working to pass reforms such as these could lead us to a more diverse Congress, one more willing to stand up to big money in politics and pass a constitutional amendment that limits campaign contributions and spending. Likewise, organizing for a constitutional amendment helps build a citizens movement that can also press for these supplemental measures as short-term victories along the way. Support for an amendment is no excuse for failing to take other steps, but neither are these measures a reason not to also demand an amendment to overturn one of the worst rulings in Supreme Court history.

What you can do: Demand answers

Ask every candidate for the US Senate whether they will block the nomination of any nominee to the federal courts who will not publicly state that unlimited campaign spending is not free speech.

Chapter 6

Magic Words

What Should a Constitutional Amendment Say?

*We do not need magic to transform our world.
We carry all of the power we need inside
ourselves already.*

—J. K. Rowling

When James Madison wrote the Bill of Rights as our first ten amendments to the Constitution, he didn't attempt to craft legislation that would cover every foreseeable situation. Rather, he laid out broad values about what our government could and could not do.

Similarly, an amendment that reins in the federal courts from voiding laws that limit campaign spending need not detail every future scenario. Rather, it must establish broad values that legislators, enforcement agencies, and courts will adhere to.

This chapter will examine several past proposals for a constitutional amendment to get big money out of politics and suggest a new one as well. These words could just as easily be incorporated into a court ruling as inserted into a constitutional amendment. Either way, the goal is to establish clear constitutional principles to guide future legislation and litigation.

The public debate and process that gets us there may be as important as the words themselves. Let's first look at language that has been introduced in the past.

The Hollings-Specter Amendment

This constitutional amendment, a bipartisan effort proposed by Democratic senator Ernest (Fritz) Hollings and Republican senator Arlen Specter during the 1980s and 1990s, said:

> *Congress shall have power to set* reasonable *limits on the amount of contributions that may be accepted by, and the amount of expenditures that may be made by, in support of, or in opposition to, a candidate for nomination for election to, or for election to, Federal office.*[149] (emphasis added)

The amendment included identical language giving states the power to set reasonable limits for state elections.

The Hollings-Specter amendment was a commonsense approach to reversing *Buckley v. Valeo.* If opponents to reform and future Supreme Court members used common sense to evaluate this amendment, it would work. However, legislative opponents to the Hollings-Specter language instead used outrageous examples of what might constitute a "reasonable" limit and said the language was too vague. In short, the opposition has not been reasonable.

Can We Please Be Reasonable?

The amendment originally introduced by Senator Hollings did not contain the word "reasonable." Senator William Roth convinced Hollings to add it to imply that judicial review would still evaluate any limits on campaign money.[150] The Fourth Amendment protects us against "unreasonable" searches and seizures by police. Senator Roth expected the courts would similarly be able to decide what was a reasonable limit based on the congressional debate outlining the purpose of the amendment. For instance, Roth explained:

> *Opponents also raised the question whether the proposal would authorize Congress to limit editorials. I must say that I never viewed editorials as campaign expenditures, and I believe that most people have the same view. If that point needed further clarification, I would think legislative history could make clear that editorial coverage is not intended to be included within the pending proposal.*[151]

Opponents were not convinced.

Senator Duncan "Lauch" Faircloth noted, "I am not a lawyer, but the term 'reasonable' seems pretty loose."[152] The ACLU claimed that "reasonable" limits on political expenditures *would* allow Congress to regulate newspaper editorials. Senator Mitch McConnell suggested that Congress could set $5,000 as a "reasonable" limit on what a challenger could spend on an entire campaign.[153] Senator Bob Bennett complained, "I cannot accept the assurance that Congress will automatically come up with what is the right definition of reasonable."[154]

But if we can't trust Congress to decide what is reasonable, do we trust the Supreme Court to do so?

Supreme Court members Antonin Scalia and Clarence Thomas issue many opinions that don't seem reasonable to many Americans. Rather than allowing future congresses and future courts to decide what is reasonable and what isn't, an amendment should specify the goals of financial campaign limits. Being more specific about the amendment's goals also can rebut the hypothetical arguments against an amendment raised by opponents.

Let's Have a Free and Fair Debate

One specific goal that an amendment could stipulate as a yardstick to measure future limits on money in politics is whether the limits serve to enhance a balanced public debate, one where many sides of an issue are heard—not just wealthy viewpoints. This goal enhances the wisdom of the crowd, as discussed in chapter 3.

Congressman Jonathan Bingham first suggested amendment language articulating the "full and free debate" rationale in 1986:

> *The Congress, having due regard for the need to facilitate full and free discussion and debate, may enact laws regulating the amounts of contributions and expenditures intended to affect elections to federal office.*[155]

It's clear that by full debate, Bingham meant complete—one where all sides were heard. But future courts might misinterpret "full" as one with no limits on any side, even if that debate became unbalanced.

During floor debates of his amendment, Senator Hollings offered fair debate as reason to limit campaign spending, noting that a huge imbalance of campaign funds meant the public only heard from one candidate while the other was effectively silenced:

> *What we are trying to do is give everybody back their freedom of speech. Namely, that I may not be extinguished by money.*[156]

In 1997, Representatives Richard Gephardt and Barney Frank introduced an amendment that built on Bingham's ideas but also fell back on the vague "reasonable" standard. It read:

> *Section 1: To promote the fair and effective functioning of the democratic process, Congress with respect to elections of Federal office, and States, for all other elections, including initiative and referenda, may adopt* reasonable *regulations of funds expended, including contributions, to influence the outcome of elections, provided that such regulations do not impair the right of the public to a full and free discussion of all issues and do not prevent any candidate for elected office from amassing the resources necessary for effective advocacy;*

> *Section 2: Such governments may* reasonably *define which expenditures are deemed to be for the purpose of influencing elections, so long as such definition does not interfere with the right of the people to fully debate issues.*[157] (emphasis added)

The Gephardt-Frank amendment struggled with drawing a line defining expenditures meant to "influence the outcome of elections." Arguably, expenditures of money to print a *New York Times* editorial could fall into this definition. A future court would likely conclude that regulating expenditures by the news media would in fact interfere with the people's right to fully debate issues and thus be impermissible under this amendment, but it would be better to be clear about this in the amendment text.

Further, the language invites a court to conclude that any reduction in spending prevents a candidate from "amassing the resources necessary for effective advocacy," as a federal court did with Washington, DC's contribution limits. It would be better to say that limits may not prevent a candidate from "amassing the resources necessary to rise to the level of notice," as the Supreme Court did in its ruling on the Missouri contribution limits.

Political Equality—The Self-Evident Truth

The Declaration of Independence observed that it was self-evident that all men are created equal. That's another good reason to limit the amount of money that any one person spends on political campaigns: to enhance political equality and create a more level playing field.

Senator Robert Byrd addressed the issue of unequal speech head-on when debating the Hollings-Specter amendment:

> *A continued failure to control campaign costs is actually what is injurious to free speech for all in political campaigns. Money has become the great "inequalizer" in political campaigns. Money talks and a lot of money talks louder than a little money. Would anyone claim that the average citizen or the small contributor has the same access to, and influence with, politicians as the major contributor or the big PAC representative? Whose opinions are heard?*[158]

In 2013, Congressman Jim McGovern introduced an amendment with language to establish equality as a reason to limit big money in politics, saying:

To advance the fundamental principle of political equality for all, *Congress shall have power to regulate the raising and spending of money and in-kind equivalents with respect to federal elections, including setting limits on (1) the amount of contributions to candidates for nomination for election to, or for election to, Federal office; and (2) the amount of expenditures that may be made by, in support of, or in opposition to such a candidate.*[159] (emphasis added)

In 2014, Senator Tom Udall combined elements of the McGovern equality language and the integrity of elections language with the "reasonable" language of Senators Hollings and Roth to arrive at the Democracy for All amendment:

To advance democratic self-government and political equality, and to protect the integrity of government and the electoral process, Congress and the States may regulate and set reasonable limits on the raising and spending of money by candidates and others to influence elections.[160]

The Democracy for All amendment would notably uphold not only limits on the size of contributions, but also the "can't vote, can't contribute" rule limiting the geography of contributions.

How to Keep Out the Press

In order to clarify that the "spending of money to influence elections" did not include newspaper editorials and similar activity, the Democracy for All amendment added, "Nothing in this article shall be construed to grant Congress or the States the power to abridge the freedom of the press."

Nonetheless, opponents to the amendment such as Senator Ted Cruz immediately did construe the amendment to do just that. It was Udall's amendment with its explicit press exemption that Cruz claimed would allow Congress to jail producers of political satire like *Saturday Night Live.*

In order to rebut the hyperbolic arguments of Senator Cruz and others, an amendment could authorize limits on "political advertising and campaigns" as a tighter description of "raising and spending money to influence elections." Nobody thinks of *Saturday Night Live* or a *New York Times* editorial as a political campaign or an advertisement even if they do involve spending money.

Should We Empower Legislators or Restrain the Courts?

Most of the amendments introduced by Congress include language granting Congress and the states the authority to set limits on campaign contributions and spending. This language suggests that this is a new power being given to the government, rather than more accurately recognizing that Congress and the states have always had this power and the courts have been wrong to restrict it.

We might also want to leave open the possibility that someone other than members of Congress should set their own campaign finance rules. As some states have done with the redistricting process, it might make sense to remove any self-interest by having an independent commission establish campaign spending and contribution limits or requiring the executive branch, or the states, to set limits for congressional races while having Congress write the rules for presidential campaigns. Inserting language authorizing only Congress to set limits for congressional races reduces our options in the long run.

"Although some see efforts to reverse *Citizens United* in the courts, or limit its effects by statute, as competing with efforts to pass a constitutional amendment, they are in fact complementary."

Representative Adam Schiff introduced an amendment that more clearly restrained the ability of courts to strike down limits without implying that government was being granted any new powers: "Nothing in this Constitution shall be construed to forbid Congress or the States from imposing reasonable content-neutral limitations on private campaign contributions or independent election expenditures."

Retired Supreme Court justice John Paul Stevens suggests something similar to Schiff, which also replaces the "expenditures to influence elections" language of many amendments with spending on "election campaigns":

Neither the First Amendment nor any other provision of this Constitution shall be construed to prohibit the Congress or any state from imposing reasonable limits on the amount of money that candidates for public office, or their supporters, may spend in election campaigns.[161]

Stevens' language, like others, still relies on the vague "reasonable" standard and fails to offer either political equality or full and fair debate as more specific metrics of what is reasonable. However, if we combine Stevens' approach with the best elements of other amendments, we arrive at this:

To advance democratic self-government and political equality, ensure a fair and balanced debate, and protect the integrity of government and the electoral process, nothing in this Constitution shall prohibit limits on the amount of money spent in, or given to, election campaigns or political advertisements.

Evolving Language

This narrowly tailored amendment is more precise than the versions that preceded it. For example, limiting money spent in election campaigns could not possibly mean censoring the news media that is purchased by the consumer in the way that regulating "expenditures to influence elections" could be. Nor would a federal bill that limited challengers to spending only $5,000 on their entire campaign, or that banned independent expenditures, further a full and fair debate. Indeed, the opposition to previous amendment proposals has strengthened this proposal—as it should have. That is, after all, the purpose of debating the issue—to lead to better public policy.

Yet these words are not magic.

Any of the above amendments could have done the job of overturning the Supreme Court's ruling in *Buckley v. Valeo*. Further refinements and perfections could have come from future court rulings interpreting and applying the amendment as well as by legislative bills and executive agency enforcement rulings that included findings as to how the amendment applied to contemporary situations.

Some activists despair that there is not one magic amendment that solves our problems of imbalanced political discourse once and for all. Rather than celebrate the many ideas put forward, these activists seek only one idea to rally the public around. While we will indeed arrive at "final" amendment language, Congress will keep perfecting the text up until a final version is proposed to the states for ratification.

History shows us that even after ratification, amendment text continues to take on new meanings as time evolves. Courts, legislatures, and executive agencies will interpret any amendment for good and for ill.

We have seen courts infer that the Fourteenth Amendment, which was passed to protect former slaves from discrimination, also protects corporations as separate "people" with rights above and beyond those of their shareholders. For a more positive example, we should look at the language of the Sixteenth Amendment, which Congress stripped of the word "progressive" to describe the income taxes it authorized. Nonetheless, Congress proceeded to enact a progressive income tax, and the Supreme Court upheld it in deference to the overall intent of the movement that passed the Sixteenth Amendment.

What If Judges Ignore an Amendment?

Even if we successfully amend "perfect" language into our Constitution, there may still be members of the Supreme Court unwilling to go along based upon their own personal ideologies. In fact, despite passage of the Sixteenth Amendment to explicitly authorize income taxes, courts during the *Lochner* era still struck down federal taxes on investment income—arguing it was only "earned income" that the amendment authorized.[162] It took the political force of Franklin D. Roosevelt to reverse that interpretation.

To make sure that errant or ideological members of the Supreme Court do not undermine or pervert the meaning of any constitutional amendment, the people need to keep the tools of defiance and impeachment sharp and ready.

Although some see efforts to reverse *Citizens United* in the courts, or limit its effects by statute, as competing with efforts to pass a constitutional amendment, they are in fact complementary. We cannot be sure which will prevail first, but we do know for sure that they are all necessary to bolster one another and ensure the long-term viability of each.

Self-government is more a journey than a destination. This does not make our walk down that path any less meaningful. Each generation of Americans will have to struggle to win and maintain the promise of political equality and the ability to conduct a full and free public debate. The price of liberty is eternal vigilance—a challenge we should not despair but should celebrate, for this struggle is what brings meaning to our collective lives and is what democracy is all about. Overturning *Citizens United* is part of this journey.

What you can do: Recruit cosponsors
Write your members of Congress and ask them to cosponsor every constitutional amendment that would overturn the *Buckley v. Valeo* ruling and authorize limits on political campaign spending.

Chapter 7

Instructions for Mission Impossible

How to Pass a Constitutional Amendment When Incumbents Don't Want One

First they ignore you, then they ridicule you,
then they fight you, then you win.

—Attributed to Mahatma Gandhi

It's one thing to amend the Constitution with something that both the public and incumbent legislators want. The Twenty-sixth Amendment, which lowered the voting age to eighteen, took only five months to pass Congress and be ratified by the states.

It's different when incumbents fear an amendment goes against their personal interests. For example, the Twenty-seventh Amendment, which prohibits a current session of Congress from raising its own pay, took 203 years from proposal to ratification.

Our mission, should we choose to accept it, is to force incumbents to do something they ordinarily wouldn't do. Our history can tell us how.

Incumbents weren't sure what would happen if they expanded the electorate by allowing women to vote. When Alice Paul got tired of waiting for Congress to act, she organized a picket outside of Woodrow Wilson's White House in 1917. Police arrested the protesters for "obstructing traffic" even though they had stayed on the sidewalk. In prison, wardens placed Alice Paul in solitary confinement. She organized a hunger strike and galvanized public support for the prisoners, who became known as the "iron-jawed angels" for refusing to be force-fed. Paul's actions elevated the issue to a national crisis and President Wilson finally came off the fence and publicly supported women's suffrage. A year later, Congress would propose the Nineteenth Amendment.

In normal times, the American public largely delegates the task of governing to our elected representatives and appointed officials. We depend on the separation of powers among the three branches of government, at both the state and federal level, to keep any one branch from becoming too powerful and straying too far from the wishes of the people.

But in extraordinary times, the People directly engage in our government. It is at these relatively infrequent moments that we change our Constitution.[163] With our busy lives, it takes a crisis to justify dropping our private concerns to focus on our government. We tend to brush aside a problem until it grows too large to ignore.

When a few activists first call for a solution, they are initially ridiculed because the problem seems too large to solve. Only when a groundswell of citizens are well along the process do opponents really engage in the debate as they begin to worry that reform might actually pass.

Once the battle is underway, victory is not far off.

Here's how that process worked with the Seventeenth Amendment, which radically changed how incumbent US senators were put in office.

Admit the Emperor Wears No Clothes

The first step in overthrowing any tyrannical regime is for a small group of courageous souls to proclaim what everyone knows but nobody dares say, namely that the current government lacks legitimacy to run the country.

That's an uncomfortable thought. It is easier to ignore it than to speak it out loud, especially for citizens of the same political party as the emperor. Nevertheless, the small group must grow to a supermajority of citizens who demand change. And that's what occurred in the years leading up to passage of the Seventeenth Amendment.

The Constitution originally called for state legislatures to appoint US senators. Calls to allow voters to directly elect senators began as early as 1826 in the House of Representatives. After the Civil War, President Andrew Johnson elevated the idea and declared that the case for direct election was so clear as to require no explanation.[164]

The problem had been identified, but we weren't ready to solve it.

First They Ignore You, Then They Ridicule You, and Only Then Do They Fight You

Until just before the turn of the twentieth century, the idea for direct election of US senators still drew little public attention. Before then, members of the House introduced constitutional amendments to provide for direct election of senators, but they went nowhere. Other issues such as slavery, settling the West, and growing the economy demanded the people's attention.

Once direct election gained traction with the public, opponents did their best to dismiss any solution as unachievable "pie in the sky."

137

As late as 1905, just seven years before the Seventeenth Amendment would pass Congress, major US newspapers dismissed the viability of direct election of senators. "We do not believe that it is possible for a long time to secure the adoption of the Amendment," said the *Wall Street Journal*.[165] The *Los Angeles Times* cynically predicted "the Senate will never willingly allow such an amendment"[166] and scoffed, "It cannot be said, with truth, that any material progress toward a realization of the proposed amendment has been made."[167]

So, you should take heart if you see a skeptical comment in today's *Los Angeles Times* about efforts to reverse *Citizens United*—it very well could mean we are only a few years away from success.

By the 1890s, Senate scandals and vacancies caused by gridlocked (and corrupt) state legislatures made the issue impossible to dismiss. Senators publicly denounced the idea of direct election, suggesting that the Senate would cease to be a deliberative body if its members had to explain themselves to voters and that "men of wisdom" would not be willing to serve if they had to go to the bother of running for office.[168]

Building State and Local Resolve

When movements are not yet strong enough to force a federal debate on an issue, activists build momentum by organizing locally. While direct election languished in Congress for decades, it gained traction in the states. California passed the first "memorial" to Congress on the issue in 1874. Wisconsin and Illinois passed resolutions supporting direct election in 1891. By 1900, thirty-three states were on record supporting the idea and a national conversation had begun.

The use of legislative resolutions to advance a national cause dates back to the colonies, which passed resolutions denouncing acts of King George in their colonial assemblies. The Declaration and Resolves of the First Continental Congress, which came two years before the Declaration of Independence, listed a set of grievances with the king. Although not legally binding, it threatened a boycott of British goods. Ten years earlier, Patrick Henry's nonbinding Stamp Act Resolutions in Virginia had established the concept that taxation was only justified if voters could elect representatives to decide how to spend taxes.

The Forgotten Practice of Voter Instructions

But sometimes voters don't want to rely only on their elected representatives to speak on their behalf through resolutions. They want to speak directly, not just as individuals but as the entire electorate—*the People*. It has been generations since Americans really thought about what it means for voters to collectively tell our elected representatives precisely how we want them to represent us. But it played a central role in passing the Seventeenth Amendment.

Constituent instructions began in England and were used by nearly all of the early American colonies prior to independence. Colonists gathered in town meetings to not only elect representatives to legislative assemblies but to specifically instruct those representatives on certain positions to take on their behalf.

Quite different from the direct democracy practiced today in twenty-four states through the initiative process, whereby citizens enact laws themselves and completely bypass legislators, the instructions process embraces the republican form of government. Instructions give elected officials clear directives on how we want them to represent us but leave the details up for our representatives to debate and finalize.

This preamble to instructions from Boston residents to their representatives in 1764 explains the idea:

> *We, the freeholders of the town, have delegated you the power of acting in our public concerns, in general as your prudence shall direct you, reserving to ourselves the* constitutional right of *expressing our minds and* giving you such instructions *upon important subjects as at any time we may judge proper.*[169] (emphasis added)

Most of the delegates at the first Continental Congress of 1774 were under instructions from their respective states. After hostilities broke out with England, at least nine of the thirteen colonies responded by instructing their delegates to the Continental Congress to declare independence.

Constituent instructions guided the drafting of the Articles of Confederation and the subsequent drafting and ratification of the US Constitution.[170] Contrary to claims that the Philadelphia Convention was a runaway constitutional convention, most delegates there were under instructions that authorized them to completely abandon the Articles of Confederation and start anew. They followed them.

In the early days of Congress, instructions from Maryland, North Carolina, South Carolina, and Virginia prodded the US Senate to conduct its meetings in public.

The Framers of our Constitution specifically mentioned the use of instructions, also known as "enjoining" a representative, as a means of amending the Constitution.

John Dickinson of Delaware, one of our Founding Fathers, explained:

> *It may perhaps be advisable, for every state, as it sees occasion, to form with the utmost deliberation, drafts of alterations respectively required by them, and to* enjoin *their representatives, to employ every proper method to obtain a ratification.*[171] (emphasis added)

As Dickinson predicted, early Americans soon used constituent instructions to prompt a constitutional amendment that reversed a Supreme Court decision they felt overstepped its bounds. Just weeks after the 1793 *Chisholm v. Georgia* decision, which ruled on a dispute between private citizens and the states, legislators in Connecticut, Massachusetts, North Carolina, and Virginia instructed their US senators to seek passage of a constitutional amendment to deny federal courts jurisdiction in such cases. Congress complied with these instructions and proposed the Eleventh Amendment, which the states soon ratified.

The Twelfth Amendment, dealing with presidential and vice presidential elections, was also prompted by instructions from Massachusetts, New Hampshire, New York, and Vermont.

The Morally Binding Power of Instructions

There has always been debate as to what extent legislators must follow their instructions. Voters cannot take a legislator to court for failing to follow instructions just as an employer cannot sue a disobedient employee. But just as your boss can fire you for not doing your job, voters can enforce instructions through removing legislators who refuse to represent them.

If instructions violate a legislator's personal views, the honorable response is to resign and allow someone else to honestly represent the views of the people. Two men who later became president, John Quincy Adams and John Tyler, did just that, resigning their seats in the US Senate rather than either follow or disobey instructions from their states.[172]

"Just as your boss can fire you for not doing your job, voters can enforce instructions through removing legislators who refuse to represent them."

Although not legally enforceable, instructions have historically proven to be morally binding. In 1883, the New York legislature placed an instructions measure on the ballot about prison labor. Citizens voted 408,402 in favor of abolishing it and 269,377 against. Rather than debating the merits of the question, the *New York Times* (which opposed abolishing prison labor) ridiculed the instruction measure, saying, "The vote will have no direct practical effect. It will be merely an expression of popular opinion, which may or may not hereafter be acted upon by the legislature."[173] Contrary to the newspaper's assertion, the vote had a great practical effect and the legislature did act upon the directions of the people.[174]

California's Constitutional Right to Instruct

Although most early states used the instructions process, eleven states saw it so fundamental to self-government that they included the right to instruct legislators, above and beyond the freedom to petition, in their state constitutions.[175]

The concept still carried weight in 1849, when California first adopted its constitution with the provision:

The people shall have the right freely to assemble together, to consult for the common good, to instruct their representatives, and to petition the legislature for redress of grievances.[176] (emphasis added)

The right to instruct was specifically added after a delegate complained that the right to petition was insufficient and that it wrongly implied that the legislature was in charge of the people, instead of the people being sovereign.[177] In debating whether legislators were bound to follow instructions, a delegate clarified the understanding:

The people have a right to instruct their representatives, and the representative has a right to refuse to obey those instructions. Both have rights. But if the representative cannot conscientiously obey those instructions, he should resign. I regard him as a mere machine, so far as he is instructed, or so far as the wishes of his constituents are known to him.[178]

Both citizens and representatives viewed individual petitions as merely "advisory" but gave greater moral authority to instructions from the entire electorate. As one elected delegate to the 1879 California constitutional convention put it, "I recognize the right of electors to petition their servants, and further, the right to instruct; and *when a majority instructs* a public servant it is his *duty to obey or resign.*"[179] (emphasis added)

Although the citizen initiative process had not yet been adopted in California, people expected the legislature to place questions on the ballot giving them the chance to instruct both their state and federal representatives. Indeed, in December 1877, the legislature placed an instructions measure on the ballot, just four months prior to calling a convention to revise the state constitution. Californians didn't vote on the measure until September 3, 1879—a few months after they had approved a new constitution, which maintained the right to instruct.

As we will see in chapter 8, all this history was forgotten 140 years later when big money interests would challenge the California legislature's decision to ask voters for instructions about overturning *Citizens United*. But in the late nineteenth century, instructions were still routine.

Voter Instructions and the Seventeenth Amendment

In 1891, the California legislature placed a voter instruction measure on the ballot asking whether US senators should be directly elected. It passed overwhelmingly with 187,987 votes in favor and 13,342 against. This was the first instruction of its kind on the direct election of senators issue and it paved the way for a more powerful measure in Oregon.

In 1901, the Oregon legislature passed a law that in effect allowed Oregon voters to directly elect their own US senators. It called for a nonbinding "straw poll" on the state ballot and for both houses of the legislature to appoint whoever won the popular vote to the Senate. This first measure failed when legislators split their votes among fourteen different candidates instead of following the straw poll.[180]

In 1907, voters in Oregon used an initiative measure to directly instruct Congress to support direct election of US senators, but also to strengthen Oregon's straw poll process.

Any legislator who did not vote to appoint the winner of the straw poll to the US Senate had a notice stating their disobedience placed under their name on their next reelection ballot. It worked. In 1909 the Oregon legislature, which was controlled by Republicans, sent a Democrat to the US Senate after he received the most popular votes, just as Oregonians had instructed.

Other states adopted Oregon's model.

In addition, many southern states had adopted primary elections where voters were allowed to specify their choice for senator. By 1908, twenty-eight of the forty-five states used some form of direct election to choose US Senate candidates who were then "ratified" by the state legislature.[181] A majority of the US Senate no longer feared direct election because they were already used to winning the votes of their constituents.

Changing the Electoral Calculus

The 1906 publication of muckraker David Graham Phillips' "Treason of the Senate" series elevated Senate elections into a national political issue that candidates needed to take a stand on. State governors joined the bandwagon and President William Howard Taft expressed support for direct election during his 1908 campaign.

The combination of overwhelming public engagement, national visibility in the news media, and a new mechanism to effectively elect senators led to an electoral upheaval. In 1910, ten senators who opposed direct election were defeated.[182]

Suddenly a senator's electoral calculus changed—he was more likely to stay in office by supporting direct election than by opposing it.

The States Force a Constitutional Crisis

Beyond the electoral tidal wave, state legislatures had forced a constitutional crisis that threatened to enact a Seventeenth Amendment through bypassing the US Senate altogether.

The Framers of our Constitution realized that Congress could have an institutional opposition to any amendment aimed at reforming itself. For this reason, Article V of our Constitution provides that state legislatures may pass an amendment without relying on Congress. Two-thirds of the states can apply for a convention, which then can draft an amendment if Congress refuses to do so.

Either way, three-quarters of states still need to ratify any proposed amendment.

Back in California, a year after its citizens had over-whelming instructed them to support direct election of senators, California legislators became the first to apply for a convention of the states to propose an amendment for direct election. By January of 1911, twenty-nine states had called for a national convention, just two states short of the two-thirds needed to convene delegates.[183]

In the end, the Senate concluded it would rather draft an amendment itself than leave it up to a convention of the states.

Senators first crafted amendments for direct election that contained various "poison pills" that they knew would ensure the amendment's defeat. This tactic survives to this day as a way to force a measure's supporters to kill it by attaching other policies that they oppose. One poison pill would have increased the size of the Senate, but the most effective would have allowed the federal government to over-see Senate elections. Southern senators who supported direct election did not want the federal government involved in their elections out of fear it would strike down poll taxes and other Jim Crow laws that prevented former slaves from voting.

Once opponents resort to the poison-pill stage of the fight, they have in effect surrendered the moral high ground and are simply delaying an inevitable victory of the movement. After two years of wrangling, a clean Seventeenth Amendment was proposed by Congress and ratified by the states.

These, then, are the historical tools we can use to limit big money in politics: resolutions to voice public opinion about the issue, voter instructions followed by electoral accountability that changes the calculus of getting elected, and finding a way to force a constitutional crisis that threatens to take the issue out of the hands of Congress or the Court if either refuses to act.

What you can do: Local instructions

Ask your city councilor to place a measure on your local ballot that instructs all elected officials to support a constitutional amendment that would overturn *Citizens United*. See appendix II for an example from Los Angeles.

Chapter 8

Halfway Home

We're Further Along Than You Think

The darkest hour is just before dawn.
—English proverb

It can be discouraging to realize that it often takes decades to overturn the Supreme Court. The good news, which we have forgotten to celebrate, is that we are already forty years into that struggle.

The first stage in repairing our Constitution from the damage of *Buckley* and *Citizens United* is for the American people to rouse ourselves out of the slumber of normal politics and enter a phase of extraordinary political engagement. Once we have corrected the structural flaws big money has wrought, we'll be able to get back to our private lives.

This first step—raising awareness—is the most time-consuming part of the amendment process. Thankfully, we are fairly well into this stage. Due in part to campaign disclosure laws, the media's muckraking, and follow-the-money groups that regularly churn out data linking campaign donations to particular issues, the American public is thoroughly aware that big money in politics is a problem. That awareness has bred disgust and cynicism, but it is only now reaching a point of anger and action.

What has been missing over the past forty years was an understanding that the US Supreme Court intentionally created this problem—and that there is a solution to that problem, namely reversing the Court with a constitutional amendment.

Admitting the Emperor Wears No Clothes

Public critique of the *Buckley* opinion began almost as soon as it was issued. Judge Skelly Wright, who had upheld the post-Watergate reforms on the appellate court, publicly disagreed with the Supreme Court's final decision.[184] However, because organizations need to demonstrate progress in order to keep their members, staff, and boards of directors motivated, most reform groups continued to tout the 1974 reforms and the pieces upheld by the 1976 court ruling in *Buckley* as a success.

Likewise, members of Congress felt they had done their job and were ready to move on to other issues. As a result, there was no supermajority support for an amendment in the 1970s or 1980s, or even public understanding that one was needed.

In June 1982, Congressman Henry Reuss of Wisconsin concluded *Buckley* was unworkable and needed to go. He introduced an amendment authorizing Congress to regulate federal campaign spending. In explaining his reasoning, he said:

> *Freedom of speech is a precious thing. But protecting it does not permit someone to shout "fire" in a crowded theater. Equally, freedom of speech must not be stretched so as to compel democracy to commit suicide by allowing money to govern elections.*[185]

In December 1982, eleven other representatives joined Reuss to back a broader amendment that authorized contribution and spending limits at both the state and federal levels.[186]

Nobody noticed.

But one of those eleven, Representative Bob Edgar from Pennsylvania, would go on to play a significant role in elevating the constitutional amendment debate.

Ignoring *Buckley*

In 1983, Reuss again introduced his amendment with bipartisan support in the House. Republican Ted Stevens from Alaska introduced it in the Senate. No hearings were held. No reform group championed the idea. Like a tree falling in a forest with nobody to hear, it made no sound.

In March 1988, the Committee on the Constitutional System, a group of several hundred current and former legislators, executive branch officials, academics, and civic leaders cochaired by President Jimmy Carter's White House counsel Lloyd Cutler, Republican senator Nancy Kassebaum, and Douglas Dillon (who served under Presidents Eisenhower, Kennedy, and Johnson), concluded:

> *The only effective way to limit the explosive growth of campaign financing is to adopt a constitutional amendment. . . . Even the Congress has found that unlimited speech can destroy the power to govern: that is why the House of Representatives has imposed time limits on Members' speeches for decades and why the Senate has adopted a rule permitting sixty senators to end a filibuster. One might fairly paraphrase Lord Acton's famous aphorism about power by saying "All political money corrupts; unlimited political money corrupts absolutely."*[187]

This committee's report became the basis of the bipartisan amendment (mentioned in chapter 6) by Senators Fritz Hollings and Arlen Specter, first introduced in 1988. Leading reformer Fred Wertheimer opposed it, saying it would only delay efforts to pass incremental reform legislation. Nonetheless, the amendment received fifty-three votes in the US Senate—still short of the sixty-seven votes needed for two-thirds support.[188]

Still, nobody noticed.

To this day, almost nobody remembers this vote even happened.

On May 27, 1993, the Senate again voted 52–43 in favor of the Hollings-Specter amendment—remarkable given that no reform organization embraced the idea and there was no media coverage of the congressional debate.[189]

Things went downhill from there.

The Stage of Ridicule: Even Reformers Oppose the Amendment

Senator Hollings would not give up. On February 14, 1995, Hollings received forty-five votes for his amendment on the floor of the US Senate.[190]

A few academics joined the fray. In 1996, Ronald Dworkin and forty other constitutional scholars signed an open letter noting:

> We believe the Buckley decision is wrong and should be overturned. The decision did not declare a valuable principle that we should hesitate to challenge. On the contrary, it misunderstood not only what free speech really is but what it really means for free people to govern themselves.[191]

By 1997, with *Buckley v. Valeo* gone from the public's consciousness, with essentially no news coverage about an amendment as a possible remedy, and with no support from major reform organizations, 59 percent of the public nevertheless supported a constitutional amendment to allow limits on campaign contributions and spending.[192]

A supermajority was forming to identify and address the problem, but pundits were not ready to take a solution seriously. In fact, the modest increase in public support only moved attention to the amendment from being ignored to being ridiculed. This was actually progress, although at the time it looked like we were taking two steps back.

In March 1997, Senator Hollings passionately took to the floor once again, telling his colleagues:

> *What* Buckley *says is: Yes, if you have a fund-raising advantage or personal wealth, then you have access to television, radio, and other media and you have freedom of speech. But if you do not have a fund-raising advantage or personal wealth, then you are denied access. Instead of freedom of speech, you have only the freedom to say nothing.*[193]

This was also the first time that any organized support existed for the amendment outside of Congress, but it was meager. As the then 28-year-old director of the Americans Against Political Corruption campaign, I was the sole advocate in Washington, DC, promoting the amendment—and I was not exactly a Beltway heavyweight. Because the Hollings-Specter amendment was one of many votes pertaining to a series of reform proposals, it was covered in national papers—but not favorably.

The *Philadelphia Inquirer* noted opposition from Common Cause, the Christian Coalition, the ACLU, and the Clinton administration and listed no supporters, while the *New York Times* quoted only the US Public Interest Research Group in support.[194] The *Buffalo News* became the first and only newspaper to endorse the amendment.[195] Senators Russ Feingold and Edward Kennedy circulated a letter saying the amendment could actually "create a permanent obstacle in the path to reform."[196]

Other Democrats used the failure of the amendment vote to launch a new effort for public financing of congressional campaigns, which they believed would be more easily won. The amendment was belittled even by many who were concerned about money in politics, who saw it as a distraction.[197]

This time only thirty-eight senators voted for the Hollings-Specter amendment, including four Republicans.

In 2000 at a Harvard Law School symposium, representatives of most reform organizations said the country didn't need an amendment.[198] Support for the amendment shrunk to thirty-three in the Senate, with Senators John McCain and William Roth as the only Republicans.

By 2001, support was back up to forty votes, including four Republicans, while big money Democrats like John Edwards and Bob Torricelli joined liberals like Edward Kennedy and Russ Feingold in opposing it.

With *Citizens United*, the Fight Begins in Earnest

Just a few years later, big money cronies smelled blood in the water. Not only was the composition of the Supreme Court more hostile to campaign limits, but support for an amendment had gone downhill in Congress. The reform movement had exhausted its energy passing the incremental McCain-Feingold bill in 2002 and then lost steam. Senator McConnell concluded that voters never punished politicians for weakening campaign finance laws, so he went on the offensive—working in broad daylight to eliminate all limits on money in politics both through legislative repeal and judicial activism.

The Supreme Court began a step-by-step dismantling of what remained of our campaign finance laws, beginning with the ruling striking down meaningful contribution limits in Vermont and continuing with the *Wisconsin Right to Life* opinion that severely weakened the McCain-Feingold law. While reform groups complained, the country hardly noticed.

All that changed with the *Citizens United* opinion.

Maybe it was the morally offensive idea of corporations being considered people with constitutional rights, combined with the idea that money was speech, although the Court had said both things before. Maybe it was the beyond-the-pale process by which John Roberts, who had promised judicial modesty in his confirmation hearings, went out of his way to issue a sweeping opinion going far beyond the facts of the case and reversing recent precedent of the Court. Maybe it was the handful of organizations that spoke out in the strongest possible terms about the decision and began organizing immediately to overturn it.

Whatever the reason, people noticed. The fight had begun.

Steeling Our Resolve

The amendment movement suddenly caught fire. Within a year of the *Citizens United* ruling, 79 percent of voters said they would support an amendment to limit corporate spending in elections, although only 22 percent knew the *Citizens United* ruling by name.[199] Just two years later, 54 percent of voters had heard of the *Citizens United* opinion,[200] possibly a higher percentage than could name any other Supreme Court case.

The amendment moved from something to ridicule and became something to fight—both for and against.

Reaction to *Citizens United* began at the grass roots, not in Washington, DC. Prominent activists formed two new organizations, Free Speech for People and Move to Amend, to organize around an amendment at the state and local level.

Just as Thomas Jefferson organized resistance to the unconstitutional federal Sedition Act by drafting state resolutions denouncing it, state legislatures led the call to repeal *Citizens United*. Hawaii was the first, passing a resolution just months after the *Citizens United* ruling "respectfully requesting" Congress to propose an amendment to clarify the distinction between the rights of persons and the rights of corporations.

I was the western states director of Common Cause at the time, and Hawaii's legislature was moving faster than the nation's oldest and largest reform organization, which still had no formal position on an amendment. Nonetheless, I told the Hawaii Common Cause director Nikki Love she could support the resolution. Things happened so fast and so organically that no other national group was even aware of Hawaii's resolution, yet it passed easily.

By this time, former Pennsylvania congressman Bob Edgar had become the president of Common Cause. As mentioned, Edgar was one of the first eleven members of Congress to support an amendment. Spurred by grassroots requests from Hawaii, Colorado, and other states, Common Cause now enthusiastically embraced the amendment, as did Public Citizen, another stalwart reform group. Organizations relatively new to campaign reform such as People for the American Way jumped on board with significant staff time and grassroots outreach. The Center for Media and Democracy was also one of the first groups to provide significant research in support of an amendment.

New Mexico became the second state. In February of 2012, the legislature passed a resolution in support of an amendment to get big money out of politics, drafted by Free Speech for People.

Faster than any one person or organization could even keep track of, let alone initiate, hundreds of state and local elected officials rose to the occasion by passing resolutions denouncing *Citizens United*. By June of 2012, five state legislatures and 288 localities had gone on record against it.

Taking It to the People

In April 2011, 78 percent of voters in Dane County, Wisconsin, approved a ballot measure drafted by Move to Amend that asked, "Should the US Constitution be amended to establish that regulating political contributions and spending is not equivalent to limiting freedom of speech, by stating that only human beings, not corporations, are entitled to constitutional rights?" In November, voters in Boulder, Colorado, and Missoula, Montana, would approve similar advisory measures by three-to-one margins.

Seeing those overwhelming results in liberal college towns, I wondered what would happen if reformers strengthened the measures to "instruct" rather than "urge" or "advise" Congress. Further, I suggested we take instruction measures to statewide electorates that were more conservative. When I floated the idea in the *Washington Monthly*,[201] many amendment proponents were skeptical. Did anyone even know what it meant to instruct our representatives? What would happen if we lost? Wouldn't that kill the movement?

Bob Edgar at Common Cause wasn't fearful. He put the full strength of the organization toward helping a statewide voter instruction measure in Montana, along with Free Speech for People and a group of local reformers who took the lead. It was a sign not only of a newer, bolder approach by Common Cause but of a reform movement that was now fully ready to embrace an idea it had marginalized during the 1990s.

Voters Issue Instructions

Montana, with its long history of standing up to big money, was an ideal battleground. The Stand with Montanans campaign formed to qualify a voter instruction and soon drew support from both Democratic governor Brian Schweitzer and Republican lieutenant governor John Bohlinger.

I-166 set an official state policy that

> *each elected and appointed official in Montana, whether acting on a state or federal level, advance the philosophy that corporations are not human beings with constitutional rights and that each such elected and appointed official is charged to act to prohibit, whenever possible, corporations from making contributions to or expenditures on the campaigns of candidates or ballot issues. As part of this policy, each such elected and appointed official in Montana is charged to promote actions that accomplish a level playing field in election spending.*[202]

In a few months, 40,092 Montanans signed petitions to place I-166 on the ballot.

Inspired by Montana's momentum, Colorado activists and organizations launched their own petition drive to qualify an instructions measure drafted by Colorado Common Cause. It said:

> *The voters instruct the Colorado congressional delegation to propose and support, and the Colorado state legislature to ratify, an amendment to the United States Constitution that allows Congress and the states to limit campaign contributions and spending, to ensure that all citizens, regardless of wealth, can express their views to one another and the government on a level playing field.*[203]

Colorado Fair Share organized an unprecedented petition drive, gathering 182,113 signatures in four short weeks—the most in Colorado initiative history.

Massachusetts has what may be the nation's oldest instructions process where signatures are gathered by legislative district. Volunteers from Common Cause, Move to Amend, and other groups qualified an instruction measure in thirty representative districts and six state senate districts, giving roughly a third of the state's voters a chance to speak their minds. It asked:

> *Shall the state representative from this district be instructed to vote in favor of a resolution calling upon Congress to propose an amendment to the U.S. Constitution affirming that (1) corporations are not entitled to the constitutional rights of human beings, and (2) both Congress and the States may place limits on political contributions and spending?*[204]

The legislature responded even before Election Day, passing a resolution calling for an amendment by a vote of thirty-five to one, with every Republican legislator in favor.

Are Words Binding?

Just as the *New York Times* had belittled nineteenth-century instructions against prison labor instead of debating the issue forthrightly, so too did opponents to the Montana and Colorado measures argue they were a waste of time because legislators weren't legally required to follow the instructions. As in the past, voters chose to instruct anyway.

In November 2012, 55 percent of Montanans voted for Mitt Romney as president, whereas 75 percent voted for I-166 to overturn *Citizens United*.[205] The country took note—the vote drew the attention of the *Wall Street Journal*[206] and praise from the *New York Times* editorial board.[207]

Voters in every Colorado county approved their instruction measure with an average of 74 percent statewide. In Massachusetts, support was at 79 percent—the same electorate gave Elizabeth Warren 53 percent of the vote.

From blue Massachusetts to red Montana, the people had spoken and the results were indisputable. Dozens of other towns and cities (including Chicago, San Francisco, and Eugene, Oregon) also passed instruction measures by overwhelming margins—usually three to one. In fact, not one instruction measure to overturn *Citizens United* has ever lost.

The unanswered question is whether voters will find a way to enforce these instructions, either by demanding legislators resign if they don't obey them or by voting out of office those who defy their constituents.

It took Oregon voters from 1901 to 1907 to effectively bind legislators to their will through the use of ballot notations that informed voters if legislators disregarded their instructions regarding specific candidates for US Senate. Success today will hinge on the ability of reformers to educate voters whether legislators have actually followed their instructions by using a different tool, since the Supreme Court has struck down ballot notations as a means to inform voters about compliance with their instructions.[208] Ironically, the Court has removed one of the tools we could use to check the Court's power.

California's Prop 49

After Richmond and San Francisco overwhelmingly passed voter instruction measures in 2012, California Common Cause approached the legislature to place an instruction measure on the statewide ballot calling for a constitutional amendment. After strong resistance from legislative staff, the bill died without even receiving a vote in its first committee.

Los Angeles moved forward, however, when the city council placed Prop C on the ballot for the spring of 2013—which 77 percent of voters passed despite opposition from the *Los Angeles Times*. (For the full text of Prop C, see appendix II.)

In 2014, I campaigned for California secretary of state on a promise to push for a voter instruction measure in 2016 to overturn *Citizens United*. The Money Out Voters In coalition thought that was too slow, so Los Angeles activist Michele Sutter began looking for a legislator to introduce a bill for the 2014 election—even though the same idea had gone nowhere just the year before.

Marianne Williamson, a prominent author, launched an outsider campaign against longtime congressman Henry Waxman on a platform that included overturning *Citizens United*. When Waxman subsequently announced his retirement, dozens of candidates entered the race, including state senator Ted Lieu. Having sponsored successful campaign disclosure bills in the past, Lieu wasn't about to be outreformed by Williamson. Further, Lieu was well aware of the instructions Los Angeles voters had given area officials in Prop C just a year before.

Lieu took up the challenge of moving an instructions bill to overturn *Citizens United* through the legislature, even though the prospects looked dim. A few months later, I thanked one of Lieu's coauthors, who acknowledged my gratitude but politely told me "it's not going to pass you know."

It looked impossible—even the bill's champions didn't think we could win.

Undeterred, the Money Out Voters In coalition—working with such organizations as the California Clean Money Campaign, Democracy for America, Courage Campaign, and CREDO Action—marshaled some 55,000 petition signatures, over 40,000 e-mails, and 176,000 faxes to California legislators in support of Senator Lieu's voter instruction measure. Hundreds of citizens attended hearings in support of the bill. In nearly twenty years of reform advocacy, I had never seen a grassroots effort this substantial.

The bill passed through committees but was still likely to die when Kai Newkirk and others from 99Rise appeared on the scene.

As noted in chapter 1, Newkirk and a dozen activists walked 480 miles from Los Angeles to Sacramento, demanding a statewide instructions vote on *Citizens United* and that the legislature immediately call for a convention with other states to begin drafting an amendment. I was one of hundreds of people who joined the march as it left Los Angeles and again when it arrived in Sacramento. The country hadn't seen anything like it since Doris "Granny D" Haddock's walk across the country in support of campaign finance reform back in 1999.

The march culminated with a rally at the California state capitol where thirteen people were arrested for protesting too long. But that was only the beginning. For two more weeks, demonstrators held teach-ins and sit-ins on the floor of the capitol rotunda—with forty-seven people eventually arrested for "speaking too much." Legislators heard their speech, with several noting the courage of "the young people" as they cast their votes for Senator Lieu's bill.

The impossible had happened and Proposition 49 was on the ballot.

The California Supreme Court Silences the People

Just as James Buckley had done in 1974, after losing in the legislature, big money sought refuge in the courts.

The Howard Jarvis Taxpayers Association knew it would not agree with what voters would say, so it tried to keep them from saying anything at all. It sued. The group argued that the legislature simply wasn't allowed to place an instruction measure on the ballot.

A district court dismissed the case almost immediately.

Then the California Supreme Court issued a stunning ruling. It removed Prop 49 from the ballot—cancelling a democratically called election. Prominent liberal judge Goodwin Liu wrote that the legislature could commission an opinion poll if it wanted to learn how voters felt about something, but it could not place an instructions measure on the ballot.

Liu and his colleagues on the California court had completely overlooked Article I, Section 3 of the California constitution, which guarantees voters the right to instruct. Our top judicial minds did not know that the California legislature had placed an instructions measure on the ballot the very same year that voters approved the state constitution. The judges' ignorance bred arrogance, and these members of the California judicial branch denied voters a chance to speak out against the federal judicial branch.

Chief Justice Tani Cantil-Sakauye, a Republican appointee, dissented. She noted that there was no harm in allowing Californians to vote on Prop 49 and the court could fully consider whether the instructions were valid in due time after the election was over, as is the normal practice of the court.

Imagine how the mainstream US media would respond if Russian president Vladimir Putin cancelled an election he was likely to lose right at the time of a major parliamentary debate.

But instead of outrage, elitist California newspapers cheered. The *Los Angeles Times*, which had opposed the local instructions measure in 2013, said Prop 49 would have "been a distraction from the consequential decisions California voters will be making on Election Day."[209] Some of those decisions included who California would send to Congress, and Prop 49 was pulled from the ballot right at the moment when Congress was taking up the issue of *Citizens United*.

Goodwin Liu was clueless about that pending congressional debate, writing "there appears to be nothing urgent on the state or federal political landscape that makes the electorate's input on *Citizens United* any more salient or timely now than it will be in, say, 2016."[210]

A Polarized Congress Renews the Debate

What Judge Liu didn't know, or bother to find out, was that after seeing the public opinion polls, the letters to the editor, the state and local resolutions, and the overwhelming voter instruction votes, Senate Majority Leader Harry Reid was finally ready to step up to the issue. He scheduled hearings and a full Senate vote on Senator Tom Udall's constitutional amendment during the summer of 2014.

Unlike the Hollings-Specter proposal, which had bipartisan support, Republican senators now unanimously rejected the amendment. Unlike the 1990s, when prominent liberal senators opposed the amendment, every Democrat now supported it.

Nearly every issue saw similar party-line votes in the 113th Congress, so the Udall vote may have hidden some true Republican supporters who didn't want to break party unity. Indeed, Republican senator Lindsey Graham came out publicly for an amendment to reverse *Citizens United* just six months later.

There may also have been some Democrats who voted in favor only to support their party and whose vote ought not to be taken for granted in the future. Nonetheless, the Senate vote could have set the stage to test whether voters would hold legislators accountable for their position on limiting money in politics. Democrats could have campaigned around

this vote and turned the 2014 elections into a national referendum on *Citizens United*.

They didn't.

Colorado senator Mark Udall followed the instructions
that his constituents passed in 2012 by voting for his cousin
Senator Tom Udall's amendment. Mark Udall's opponent,
Cory Gardner, dodged taking a position on the *Citizens
United* ruling.[211] Yet Udall didn't run a single ad about his
position on *Citizens United* and instead focused on abortion.
Mark Udall lost.

Voters gave Republicans control of the US Senate shortly
after every Republican senator voted against the amendment. Although some candidates and outside groups did
raise the issue of corruption,[212] the election was not about
Citizens United or a constitutional amendment. Unlike the
election of 1936, where voters clearly considered and rejected
the Supreme Court's repudiation of the New Deal, the 2014
elections were a general rejection of President Obama's han-
dling of the economy and foreign policy. Obama's approval
rating was at 40 percent, and a majority of the country was
pessimistic about the future.

Democratic candidates may not have campaigned
around the Udall amendment because reformers and reporters tend to portray both parties as equally corrupt. Campaign disclosure laws do indeed reveal that candidates from
both parties accept huge funds from special interests. Alter-
natively, some Democratic candidates may not have wanted
to alienate their own big money donors during the
campaign.

So while voters were upset by big money in politics, they
did not yet perceive that either major party would deliver a

solution in 2014. That may be why record numbers of voters stayed home on Election Day.

Perhaps that will change in 2016 as Bernie Sanders, Hillary Clinton, and other Democrats made overturning *Citizens United* a priority, both with support for a constitutional amendment and pledging to appoint justices who would overturn it to the Supreme Court.

Changing the Electoral Calculus

In a 1995 letter to his House Republican colleagues, who were increasingly supportive of limiting money in politics, Senator Mitch McConnell reminded them that they had killed campaign finance reform right before the 1994 elections and yet taken over the House majority that year. That was "proof positive that this issue is not a hindrance to us at the polls," McConnell concluded.[213] The 2014 elections only reinforced his view.

Republican voters want to limit big money in politics by nearly the same huge margins as Democratic or Independent voters. But some Republican legislators, McConnell in particular, have calculated that there is a greater advantage to be gained by accepting huge contributions and opposing limits than any downside of losing support from voters. Reformers will not win until that calculus changes in one (or all) of three ways:

1. Democrats could go for the money by adopting pro-Wall Street stances and other corporate positions in an attempt to outraise Republicans. For instance, Congress agreed to ban soft money to national parties at about the time Democrats had reached parity with

Republicans in soft money fund-raising. Some Democrats are indeed pursuing this strategy, arguing that Democrats need to become more pro-corporate in order to be competitive.[214] Tom Steyer, a billionaire investment banker who favors Democratic candidates and causes, spent $74 million of his own money to influence the 2014 elections, more than any other single person. To the extent that Democrats succeed in at least tying the fund-raising arms race, we may see more Republican legislators supporting an amendment and perhaps fewer Democrats. This would also reduce any chance that voters will perceive a difference between the parties on the issue of big money in politics.

2. Voters could punish candidates of any party for their positions on *Citizens United* by voting them out of office, changing the calculus that it is more valuable to raise big money than to side with constituents. Voters are only likely to do this if there are stark differences between candidates on the issue of *Citizens United*, if voters are aware of those differences, and if they believe that an amendment can pass and will work. Unless one party can truly distinguish itself as the party of reform, voters may be more likely to prioritize campaign spending limits as an issue in primary elections, between candidates of the same party who hold similar positions on other issues.

3. Underdog candidates of both parties could find a way to win even while being outspent, thus reducing the advantages of big money. This could happen if candidates take populist positions that bring new voters into the electorate, if either the mainstream news media or

social media plays a greater role than paid ads in informing voters about candidates' positions, or if grass-roots candidates find ways to compete with big money candidates through free airtime, voters guides, public financing, or small donor contributions.

The Fate of the 49ers

On October 5, 2015, the California Supreme Court finally conducted a thorough hearing of the merits of Prop 49, which it had preliminarily removed from the ballot in 2014 on the grounds that it would likely be found unconstitutional. Free Speech for People submitted an amicus brief on behalf of the Money Out Voters In coalition and several public interest groups. The brief reminded the court of California's constitutional guarantee of the right to instruct and of the clear understanding by voters that legislators would refer instructions to the ballot.

As this book goes to print, the California court still has not ruled on the appeal of Proposition 49. Californians may yet get the chance to instruct their congressional delegation to amend the constitution to get big money out of politics.

What If They Won't Let Us Instruct?

California is not the only place where judges and other bureaucrats try to prevent people from having a direct say in their government. Many city attorneys turn up their nose at the idea of using the ballot to further a national conversation about any issue. Ignoring that a constitutional amendment requires a massive conversation above and beyond normal politics, the bean counters want to focus only on the trees without stepping back to look at the forest.

It's often possible to surmount bureaucratic opposition to a voter instruction by combining it with other ideas. For instance we could:

- enact an official policy, as Montana and San Francisco did in 2012, and then instruct all elected officials to implement the policy, or

- require an elected official, perhaps the secretary of state, to transmit the results of the instruction to all elected representatives in the state and then report back to voters on whether legislators carried out those instructions, or

- combine instructions with a jurisdiction-wide Democracy Day where public officials are required to conduct a hearing on the general status of democracy and specifically on whether legislators have complied with instructions, or

- pass a statute that limits money in politics in direct defiance of the US Supreme Court and also instruct elected officials to use all their official capacity and authority to enforce that statute.

Next Steps

Before it succeeds, the amendment movement will enter a stage where it finds majority support in both houses of Congress but not the two-thirds necessary to send an amendment to the states to ratify. It has already reached that stage in the US Senate. This stage will be similar to the 1890–1911 period during the movement to win direct election of senators, when there was supermajority support among the public and two-thirds support in the House but not in the Senate. Here are seven steps reformers could take to convert supermajority public support into sufficient legislative support.

Step 1: A Confirmation Battle Royale

The next president will likely have the opportunity to replace at least one Supreme Court member who opposed *Citizens United* (perhaps Ruth Bader Ginsburg) and two members who supported it (possibly Anthony Kennedy and Antonin Scalia). If two out of those three new members oppose the *Citizens United* ruling, *and* if a new case is presented to the court before the vote count flips back, the Court could reverse *Citizens United* on its own. The confirmation process alone could turn into a national debate about big money in politics. Americans should demand that senators ask Court nominees whether they think unlimited spending is the same thing as free speech and oppose confirmation of any nominee who provides a squishy answer. Voters could also question candidates for the Senate to see if they would apply this litmus test to court nominees.

Step 2: A National Voter Instruction

Citizens in Alaska, Arkansas, and Washington state may follow the lead of Colorado and Montana and hold statewide votes to instruct their congressional delegation to use all possible means to overturn the *Citizens United* ruling, including a constitutional amendment. Other states may join the effort—but many states do not have a process by which citizens can place an instruction question on the ballot.

So why not do it nationally? Unlike in California and other states, there is no national right to instruct members of Congress, nor is there a national initiative process where voters can place questions on the ballot. But nothing prohibits Congress from placing a voter instruction measure on the national ballot just as Chicago, Los Angeles, San Francisco, and other localities have done.[215] Reformers could take this step with majority support that falls short of the two-thirds needed to formally move an amendment out of Congress.

Although we have never had a national instructions vote, the idea has been proposed before. Senator William Stone introduced a bill for a national voter instruction measure in 1916 to ascertain the people's wishes about entering World War I.[216] In 1939, the House actually voted on a similar proposal by Wisconsin senator Bob La Follette regarding World War II, defeating it by vote of seventy-three to seventeen.[217]

It's unclear if Congress could force state election officials to place a federal instruction question on state ballots. If a state refused, Congress could direct the Election Assistance Commission or another federal agency to administer the instruction election using a separate vote-by-mail ballot.

Step 3: Defy the Roberts Court

Either a federal instruction measure or a state ballot initiative could combine a voter instruction with a statute that defies the Supreme Court's edict that money is speech—for instance by setting limits on contributions to super PACs or on candidate campaign spending. That would set the stage either for a court reversal or a constitutional crisis if the executive branch chose to enforce the law despite the Supreme Court's contrary opinion.

In 2012, Representative John Dingell introduced a defiance bill called the Restoring Confidence in Our Democracy Act that reenacted the policies that the Roberts Court struck down in *Citizens United*. Congress could pass a similar bill by majority vote.

John Roberts does not want to go down in history as the chief justice who baited Congress to ignore him and permanently weaken the Supreme Court as an institution. He also doesn't want to find out what would happen if a president refused to send in troops to enforce his Court's unjust order against a state law limiting money in politics.

Reformers will win if John Roberts concludes now what Owen Roberts concluded in 1937 when he made the "switch in time that saved nine" described in chapter 5—that the only way to preserve his institution's power and his place in history is to reverse his wrongheaded ruling.

Step 4: A New Electoral Strategy for Uniform Accountability

In 2014, Harvard professor Larry Lessig formed a project called the Mayday PAC, which spent more than $10 million in ten targeted races around the country trying to elect reformers and defeat antireform incumbents. While the effort no doubt influenced some voters, it neither persuaded enough of them to prioritize reform as an issue, nor inspired many new people to enter the electorate.

One factor that thwarted Mayday PAC was that incumbent political machines moved big money into the ten targeted races in order to offset Mayday's spending. Some critics questioned the choice of targets as well.

Rather than targeting a handful of races, reformers could apply uniform criteria to all races and issue a scorecard to every incumbent and a corresponding pledge to every challenger on whether they would support a constitutional amendment to reverse *Citizens United*. Moving a small number of voters to prioritize this issue in every district might be easier than getting a larger number to prioritize the issue in a small number of districts.

With low-turnout elections where very few voters change their minds, changing just a few votes in a district that was not targeted could yield surprising results. This strategy could work particularly well in primary elections, just as the Tea Party has demonstrated success in unseating incumbents who have not addressed their priorities and concerns. An electoral campaign would work even better if there has been a national instructions measure to which every incumbent can be held accountable.

Step 5: Changing the Process State by State

One of the key factors in winning direct election of senators and women's suffrage was the ability of reformers to change the rules at the state level. Members of Congress from those states then had no reason to fear new federal rules because they were already playing under similar state rules.

The 1974 Federal Election Campaign Act (FECA) preempted states from setting their own contribution limits for congressional elections. Courts have ruled that this same preemption prevents states from offering public financing to federal candidates. But this part of FECA could be repealed.

Reformers who had a simple majority, but not two-thirds, could abandon a uniform federal approach and go back to letting states set rules for their own congressional races. We might then see several states sending members to Congress who could only accept small contributions rather than the current federal limit of $2,700. Especially if those states matched small contributions with public funds, some grassroots candidates would be able to beat big money candidates backed by the super PACs.

Even without a repeal of FECA, states could implement digital voter guides that provide every candidate an opportunity to communicate with voters at no cost to their campaign through a series of online videos. California and other states already provide voters with printed guides to candidates for federal office, which does not conflict with federal campaign finance rules.

Step 6: Forcing a Crisis with a Convention of the States

A grassroots group called Wolf PAC is leading efforts to have legislatures apply for a convention of the states to draft an amendment if Congress refuses to do so. They have had impressive success, with Vermont, California, Illinois, and New Jersey making formal applications for a convention and other states seriously considering it.

Several questions about how a convention would work have hindered this approach, including:

- ◆ Who will be the delegates to the convention?
- ◆ What will the rules be for the convention?
- ◆ Will it be confined to proposing amendments only on one topic, or can delegates propose multiple amendments about anything they want?

A significant push for a convention of states to propose a balanced-budget amendment has demonstrated the power of this approach, but it has also raised concerns. Since the 1980s, some twenty-seven states have applied for a convention to draft a balanced-budget amendment, and that momentum (combined with Ross Perot's presidential run) pressured a Republican Congress and President Bill Clinton to enact several balanced budgets in the 1990s. States are renewing these efforts, leading those who worry about the damage a balanced budget could do during times of war or recession to oppose *any* constitutional convention for fear it could produce a balanced-budget amendment in addition to other amendments.

Congress could resolve such questions, again by majority vote, and pass rules by which a convention of state delegates would operate. But Congress has refused to do this because it does not want to encourage a convention of states around any issue. Nonetheless, if a simple majority in Congress was really serious about an amendment to limit big money in politics, it could take this step.

An alternative would be for the states calling for a convention to pass what's known as an interstate compact that would set the rules for the convention to operate. Interstate compacts are routine procedures that often deal with issues such as regional transit authorities or bodies of water that cross state lines.

There is a growing movement to change the way states appoint their representatives to the Electoral College through an interstate compact that would in effect institute a national popular vote for presidential elections.[218] Interstate compacts are guaranteed in the Constitution and enforceable in court.

A state's compact for a convention could specify who delegates would be—perhaps the Speaker of each house from a state's legislature as well as the leaders of the majority and minority parties. It could include a provision to immediately recall a state's delegates if any member of the convention proposed an amendment that was beyond the scope that had been authorized by the state applications. In that way, legislatures could prevent the convention from going off topic by denying it a quorum.

Most likely, as with the Seventeenth Amendment, Congress would act once the number of states calling for a convention approached the number needed to actually convene one. But if Congress still stonewalled, the states' convention could propose an amendment that would still require ratification of thirty-eight state legislatures.

That ratification requirement, along with an interstate compact or congressional rules outlining precisely how the convention would operate, would eliminate concerns about a runaway convention proposing amendments a supermajority of voters do not want.

Step 7: Nonviolent Protest

Supreme Court rulings are not set in stone. They are not brought down from the mountaintop by Moses, John Roberts, or anyone else. They are not always right.

As a government becomes more tyrannical, it closes off formal processes for change and dissent. Judges ignore state constitutions in order to cancel voter instruction elections aimed at refuting other judges, for instance.

Too often, reformers confine their imagination to the narrow box of prescribed rules for passing policy rather than stepping back to the inherent and inalienable rights set forth in our Declaration of Independence. When we find our formal process for governing ourselves is broken, we can do what people the world over have done to overthrow corrupt and oligarchic regimes.

We can take to the streets.

Our predicament is less dire than what workers in Poland's Solidarity movement faced in the 1980s, or what blacks living under South Africa's apartheid regime endured for almost fifty years. Pro-democracy activists in Egypt did not change their constitution by following the rules outlined by Hosni Mubarak; they ousted him with protests in Tahrir Square. If they can prevail, so can we.

Nonviolent direct action has deep roots in the United States. Although polite advocacy played an important role in winning the right to vote for women, suffrage was pushed over the brink when the "iron-jawed angels" refused to be force-fed. Their hunger strike spoke louder than words when the government imprisoned them for their political speech.

Our Supreme Court tries to project power, but it does not command any army and lately does not command much public respect. The 320 million residents who are not on the Supreme Court can easily defeat the five recalcitrant ideologues who control the Court.

Just such a popular protest movement is already afoot.

One year after Kai Newkirk was arrested for speaking his mind in the US Supreme Court, seven more people were jailed for doing the same thing. Four months later, on the one-year anniversary of the *McCutcheon v. FEC* ruling, five more members of 99Rise were arrested for protesting inside the Supreme Court despite escalating threats of prosecution.

On April 15, 2015, Florida mailman Doug Hughes risked his life by flying his gyrocopter through restricted airspace to land on the lawn of the US Capitol. Hughes was arrested before he could deliver his 535 letters to members of

Congress demanding that they overturn the *Citizens United* ruling. More such protests—equally disruptive, equally creative—are sure to follow.

The jails cannot hold 320 million people. What will they do when they run out of space?

Why It Is Easier to Accomplish a More Daunting Task

Pundits who are closer to the mechanics of passing legislation than they are to the desires of the people think it is easier to pass a modest reform statute than a sweeping constitutional amendment. After all, it takes sixty-seven votes in the US Senate to propose an amendment compared to only sixty votes to break a filibuster and pass legislation.

But, is there a scenario where it is easier to get to sixty-seven than it is to get to sixty? Only if the proposal that needs sixty-seven votes musters significantly more public support than the incremental proposal—and this is the situation we find ourselves in with a constitutional amendment to get big money out of politics.

Joe Biden, in explaining his support for an amendment in addition to incremental reforms, noted that "moderate reform is like moderate chastity."[219]

It is difficult to persuade citizens to devote the time and energy needed to win any reform if it doesn't seem as if it will make much of a difference. Likewise, voters will prioritize other issues instead of money in politics when casting their ballots if the differences between candidates are only a matter of degree or if every candidate can claim to be "anti-corruption" but not held to any simple yet specific standard of what that means. And of course, no protester will risk arrest, let alone being shot out of the sky, just to pass a minor disclosure provision in wonky campaign finance law.

To reach either sixty-seven or sixty votes in the US Senate, reformers will need support from both Republican and Democratic legislators. It may actually be easier to get fifteen or twenty members of a political party to support a simple and popular amendment all together than it would be to get only four or five to break ranks over an obscure incremental measure that the public does not understand.

Along the way to an amendment, reform opponents will try to ventilate public pressure by offering partial solutions.

That's good, because pressure for a real solution won't go away, and we are more likely to win incremental victories by thinking big than by using incremental measures as a starting point for negotiations.

Reform Springs Eternal

When I first began working on money in politics in the mid-1990s, I figured we'd "solve" our problems in five to ten years and then I could go on to other things.

Like most reformers, I was drawn to the issue because I saw how big money had influenced and corrupted issues that had a direct impact on my life. When I realized it might take more than five to ten years, I drew up a twenty-year plan. But regardless of the timeline, it was important to me that there was a goal in sight, some time when the work would be done.

Five years into my work, my outlook changed. I found myself in Siena, Italy, inside one of the oldest city halls in existence. The people who had lived there formed city-states that operated as democracies hundreds of years before the American Revolution. Our Founders drew inspiration and experience from those Italian city-states.

Inside the 700-year-old city hall of Siena there is an extensive set of murals depicting good government and bad government. In the bad government painting, corruption flourishes, while famine and plague sweep the countryside.

While viewing the mural, I realized that reforming government is not a finite project. Reform will never be completed but is rather an ongoing process that every generation must undertake. We form a government only to see it change its form. We then must form it again—reform springs eternal.

We cannot inherit self-government from our forefathers; we must take it upon ourselves to achieve it.

It can be depressing to realize that we will never permanently arrive at "good" government and will instead forever strive for "better" government than we currently have. But, this realization is also encouraging. Even if our work is never done, we know that things can and will get either better or worse depending upon our own actions.

Doctors know that eventually every patient they treat will die, but the quality and length of their life can often be improved by diligent medical care, or shortened by neglect. Likewise, citizens must accept that there will be continual threats to our democratic republic, but with diligence and commitment we can make things better.

If we don't act, we can also be assured that things will get worse.

It is up to us.

What *you* can do: To each her own

Pick one of these steps that's right for you, and let others do the same. Different reformers prefer different means of solving the same problem, and that diversity is an asset. We don't know which tactic will prevail, but we do know that having every citizen engage the problem will make every solution more likely. So, rather than arguing with fellow Americans about whether it's best to focus on the courts, push Congress for an amendment, or call for a convention to propose an amendment, just move forward with the approach that you prefer.

Epilogue

by Miles Rapoport

Money in politics is nothing new. But the current dominance of big dollar donors, their identities and motives largely hidden from public view, is a new and dangerous development for American democracy.

As Derek Cressman describes in this book, the trouble goes back to the Supreme Court's 1976 ruling in *Buckley v. Valeo*, which first equated money with speech. The justices made things worse with their 2010 decision in *Citizens United*.

Rather than uniting citizens, as the name of that infamous ruling might imply, the decision reflected a Court majority united *against* citizens. Rather than protecting democracy, Chief Justice Roberts and his allies are serving the wealthiest and most powerful among us.

It is not just in campaign finance that the Roberts Court is undercutting democracy. The Court in 2013 struck a blow against the Voting Rights Act, in *Shelby County v. Holder*. In 2014, it extended the logic of its holding that corporations are people in the *Hobby Lobby* case, ruling that a corporation could use a claim of religious freedom to evade the Affordable Care Act. I believe that all these decisions will one day be spoken of in the same breath as the infamous

Dred Scott decision, and will be reconsidered and overturned by a future Supreme Court.

Past Supreme Courts have had many justices with experience in governing and campaigning. Earl Warren was governor of California prior to serving as chief justice; Sandra Day O'Connor was a former Arizona state legislator. None of today's justices have experience running for or serving in office. Their lack of understanding of the other branches of our government is telling.

The Roberts Court has upheld restrictions on state judges personally asking for campaign funds, correctly reasoning that such contributions could taint the public's view of the judiciary. But Chief Justice Roberts apparently sees no problem with legislators raising huge sums of money or benefiting from unlimited campaign spending by corporations and billionaires. It is as if he and his brethren expect our politicians to be corrupt and see no point in trying to prevent it.

Polls have consistently shown that strong majorities of Democratic, Republican, and Independent voters support limits on political spending. The politicians are beginning to get the message. Democrats Hillary Clinton and Bernie Sanders, as well as Republican Lindsey Graham, highlighted their opposition to *Citizens United* in the early stages of their 2016 presidential campaigns.

With public opinion overwhelmingly on our side, the question is how long must democracy suffer before the Supreme Court's mistake is corrected. It will require a determined, sustained effort, but the goal—a constitutional amendment overturning *Citizens United* and permitting reasonable regulations on political spending—is within reach.

When Senate Majority Leader Mitch McConnell spoke to a room full of billionaires convened by the industrialists Charles and David Koch, he reportedly told them that the worst day in his political life was when then President George W. Bush signed the McCain-Feingold law, which limited independent political spending.

Senator McConnell has called a constitutional amendment to overturn *Citizens United* radical; it is anything but. In a few sentences, we can restore an understanding of the Constitution that was in place for at least a century until recently unraveled by the Supreme Court. An amendment would simply reaffirm what we all know—that money is not speech and that no one, however wealthy or powerful, has a constitutional right to spend unlimited sums to influence our elections.

McConnell argues that proposals to limit political spending are aimed at silencing critics of government. Nonsense. As Derek Cressman has explained, limiting campaign money would protect the First Amendment; every citizen's right to express their views, however unpopular or unconventional, would remain intact.

The real radicals are those who argue that their free speech rights are a license to use wealth to drown out the voices of other Americans and buy our elections. They view the *Citizens United* decision as having, in Senator McConnell's words, "level[ed] the playing field" for corporations.

Americans know better. Already, sixteen states and some 650 localities have called on Congress to send the states a constitutional amendment overturning *Citizens United*. In two states, Colorado and Montana, voters sent the message directly, through ballot measures that Derek

Cressman helped lead when he was a vice president at Common Cause. We can thank Derek for his early, strategic thinking and organizing that built momentum for a constitutional amendment as the *people's* solution to the problem.

In the fall of 2014, fifty-four senators cast votes signaling their support for an amendment, effectively declaring that big ideas, not big money, should rule in the public square. The vote was a historic milestone, but much remains to be done to secure the two-thirds majority in Congress that would send the amendment to the states for ratification.

When Money Talks calls on all of us to reflect on what has gone wrong with our elections. Now comes the time for action. As Common Cause's founder John Gardner said years ago:

> *Our society must have the wisdom to reflect and the*
> *fortitude to act. It must provide the creative soil for*
> *new ideas and the skill and patience and hardihood to*
> *put those ideas into action.*[220] (emphasis original)

This book contains many ideas, new and old, for action. It is up to us to find the skill, patience, and determination to carry those ideas forward. A plethora of organizations, Common Cause among them, are pursuing different approaches to solving the problem of big money in politics. These groups are listed in appendix I. Some are focusing on improving disclosure of political spending and using public funds to augment the role of small donors; others are leading the fight for a constitutional amendment. It's all important work. I hope you'll search out the organizations that best suit you, and then roll up your sleeves and get to work.

Appendix I

Resources and Organizations

Updated information and a free download of three bonus chapters to this book can be found at www.WhenMoney Talks.com. You can also contact author Derek Cressman at this site and sign up for regular updates.

Here are some organizations that are working to pass a constitutional amendment to get big money out of politics (see also www.United4thePeople.org for updates to this list and a clearinghouse of activity):

99Rise: www.99rise.org
Center for Media and Democracy: www.prwatch.org
Common Cause: www.commoncause.org
The Courage Campaign: www.couragecampaign.org
CREDO Action: www.credoaction.com
Democracy Initiative: www.democracyforus.org
Demos: www.demos.org
Every Voice: www.everyvoice.org
Free Speech for People: www.freespeechforpeople.org
Money Out Voters In coalition: www.moneyoutvotersin.org
Move to Amend: www.movetoamend.org
People for the American Way: www.pfaw.org
Public Citizen: www.citizen.org
Reclaim the American Dream: www.reclaimtheamerican dream.org
Stamp Stampede: www.stampstampede.org
US PIRG: www.uspirg.org
Wolf PAC: www.wolf-pac.com

Appendix II

Sample Voter Instruction Measure from Los Angeles

See www.WhenMoneyTalks.com for the text of other measures, including from Colorado, Massachusetts, Montana, and San Francisco, as well as California's Proposition 49.

The resolution reprinted here placed a measure on the May 2013 ballot in the city of Los Angeles. Titled Proposition C, it received 77 percent of the vote.

Resolution providing that a ballot measure be submitted to the qualified voters of the City of Los Angeles.

Be it resolved by the Council of the City of Los Angeles as follows:

Section A. The following resolution of the people of the City of Los Angeles is hereby proposed to be submitted to the qualified voters of the City of Los Angeles at a Special Election to be called on May 21, 2013 and consolidated with the City's General Municipal Election on the same date:

RESOLUTION

WHEREAS, the First Amendment to the United States Constitution was designed to protect the free speech rights of human beings, not corporations, and,

WHEREAS, the Unites States Constitution never mentions the word corporations; and

WHEREAS, corporations can and do make important contributions to our sociey using powerful advantages that government has wisely granted them, but that does not make them real people; and

WHEREAS, the U.S. Supreme Court's 5–4 ruling in *Citizens United v. Federal Election Commission* rolled back legal restrictions on corporate spending in the electoral process, allowing unlimited corporate spending to influence elections, candidate selection, and policy decisions, thereby threatening the voices of citizens and the foundation of our democracy; and,

WHEREAS, the opinion of the four dissenting justices in *Citizens United* noted that corporations have special privileges not enjoyed by real people, such as limited liability, perpetual life, and favorable treatment of the accumulation and distribution of assets, that allow them to spend huge sums on campaign messages that have little or no correlation with the beliefs held by real people; and,

WHEREAS, the *Citizens United* decision supercedes certain important state and local efforts to regulate corporate activity in their elections; and,

WHEREAS, the United States Supreme Court held in *Buckley v. Valeo* (1976) that the appearance of corruption justifies some limits on contribuitons to candidates, but it wrongly rejected other fundamental interests such as creating a level playing field and ensuring that all citizens, regardless of wealth, have an opportunity to have their political views heard; and,

WHEREAS, the people of the United States have previously used the constitutional amendment process to correct those egregiously wrong decisions of the United States Supreme Court that go to the heart of our democracy and self-government; and

NOW, THEREFORE, BE IT RESOLVED that the people of the City of Los Angeles instruct the Los Angeles Congressional Delegation to propose and support any joint resolution offering an amendment to the United States Constitution that accomplishes the following:

Overturns all portions of the United States Supreme Court's rulings in *Buckley v. Valeo* (1976) and *Citizens United v. FEC* (2010) that conflict with the following objectives: (1) Corporations do not have the constitutional rights of human beings; and (2) corporations do not engage in constitutionally protected speech when spending corporate money to influence the electoral process; and (3) limits on political spending that promote the goals of the First Amendment, by ensuring that all citizens—regardless of wealth—have an opportunity to have their political views heard, are permissible.

BE IT FURTHER RESOLVED that the people of the City of Los Angeles instruct the Los Angeles Congressional delegation to work diligently to bring such a joint resolution to a vote and passage, and to use all procedural methods available to secure a vote and passage;

BE IT FURTHER RESOLVED that the people of the City of Los Angeles instruct each state legislator representing Los Angeles residents, if given the opportunity, to ratify any amendment to the United States Constitution that is consistent with the purposes and findings expressed in this resolution.

This resolution shall take effect immediately.

Notes

1. Associated Press, "FEC Chair All but Giving Up Hope to Rein in Money Abuses," *New York Times*, May 2, 2015, http://www.nytimes. com/aponline/2015/05/02/us/politics/ap-us-fec-chair.html?_r=0.

2. Thomas Jefferson letter to William Charles Jarvis, September 28, 1820.

3. Thomas Jefferson letter to Samuel Kercheval, July 12, 1816.

4. See the Alliance for Justice report, "The Roberts Court and Judicial Overreach," for details, http://www.afj.org/wp-content/uploads/2013 /09/the-roberts-court-and-judicial-overreach.pdf.

5. The Center for Responsive Politics found that from 2000–2010, the candidate for the House of Representatives who spent the most money won 93 percent of the races. See http://www.opensecrets.org/news /2012/01/big-spender-always-wins/.

6. See http://www.acrreform.org/research/money-in-politics-who -gives/ in reference to the 2008 election. This data is difficult to quantify because federal contributions of under $200 are not reported—only the aggregate total of money raised from these donors is known. See also "A Brief History of Money In Politics," Center for Responsive Politics, 1995, noting 8 percent of adults contributed to candidates in 1968, but that had fallen to 4 percent in 1992.

7. "Donor Demographics," Center for Responsive Politics, https://www.opensecrets.org/overview/donordemographics.php.

8. "Billion-Dollar Democracy," Demos and US PIRG, January 17, 2013, http://www.uspirg.org/reports/usp/billion-dollar-democracy.

9. David Callahan and J. Mijan Cha, "Stacked Deck," Demos, February 2013, http://www.demos.org/stacked-deck-how-dominance-politics-affluent -business-undermines-economic-mobility-america.

10. The term "wealth primary" was coined by Jamin Raskin and John Bonifaz in the 1992 *Yale Law and Policy Review* article, "Equal Protection and the Wealth Primary."

11. According to reports filed with the California Secretary of State, Tim Donnelly raised $73,985 from donors giving under the $100 reporting threshold. Neel Kashkari raised only $7,904 from small donors during his entire primary campaign.

12. *Field Poll*, Release #2463, March 18–April 5, 2014, http://field.com/fieldpollonline/subscribers/Rls2463.pdf.

13. Donnelly was polling at 15 percent and Kashkari at 10 percent in a survey by the Public Policy Institute of California from May 8–15, 2014, http://www.ppic.org/main/pressrelease.asp?i=1531.

14. See https://www.gutenberg.org/wiki/Gutenberg:About.

15. The Richmond City Council meeting on February 7, 2012, adjourned at 11:41 p.m. according to the council's rules and procedures after a motion to extend the meeting by forty-five minutes had been approved. Nonetheless, there wasn't sufficient time for the council to discuss a ballot measure calling upon Congress to support a constitutional amendment to overturn the *Citizens United* case. See http://www.ci.richmond.ca.us/ArchiveCenter/ViewFile/Item/4305.

16. See http://www.redcross.org/what-we-do/disaster-relief/hurricane -recovery-program.

17. See http://www.washingtontimes.com/news/2004/oct/21/20041021 -113328-4826r/?page=all.

18. See http://presidentialrecordings.rotunda.upress.virginia.edu/essays ?series=. Most accounts claim that the president made this statement to Bill Moyers following the signing of the Civil Rights Act. See Bill Moyers, "Second Thoughts: Reflections on the Great Society," *New Perspectives Quarterly* 4 (Winter 1987); Jan Jarboe, "Lady Bird Looks Back: In Her Own Words, A Texas Icon Reflects on the Lessons of a Lifetime," *Texas Monthly* (December 1994), p. 117; and "Achilles in the White House: A Discussion with Harry McPherson and Jack Valenti," *Wilson Quarterly* 24 (Spring 2000), p. 92.

19. Indeed, incrementalism in England not only improved the lives of slaves but eventually and gradually did result in the end of slavery in England. See http://abolition.e2bn.org/people_24.html.

20. Karen Graham, "Judge Tells BP Lawyers: This Is Not a College Term Paper," *Digital Journal*, September 17, 2014, http://www.digitaljournal.com/news/environment/judge-tells-bp -lawyers-this-is-not-a-college-term-paper/article/403788.

21. See, for instance, *Village of Schaumburg v. Citizens for a Better Environment,* US Supreme Court, 1980.

22. See http://drivinglaws.aaa.com/laws/motorcycle-noise-limits/ for a list of laws regulating motorcycle noise.

23. The US Supreme Court upheld a ban on "loud and raucous noises," even as applied to political sound trucks, in the 1949 case *Kovacs v. Cooper.*

24. Associated Press, "3 Arrested at Protest against NC Gay-Rights Group," *Charlotte Observer*, November 24, 2014, http://www.charlotteobserver.com/2014/11/23/5337184/3-arrested -at-protest-against.html?sp=/99/115/141/#.VKHnDV4AAA.

25. See Jonathan Lloyd and Jason Kandel, "More than 100 Ferguson Protestors Arrested on Third Night of Demonstrations," NBC, November 27, 2014, as an example of arrests in Los Angeles: http://www.nbclosangeles.com/news/local/Los-Angeles-Ferguson -Grand-Jury-Protest-Michael-Brown-LAPD-283991451.html.

26. Christina Bellantoni, *Talking Points Memo*, December 5, 2009, http://talkingpointsmemo.com/dc/strange-scene-10-arrested-as -tea-partiers-heckle-police.

27. Christine May-Duc, *Los Angeles Times*, October 3, 2004, http://www.latimes.com/nation/nationnow/la-na-nn-guantanamo -videotapes-20141003-story.html.

28. Assange is quoted in *Time*, December 1, 2010, http://content.time.com/time/specials/packages/article/0,28804 ,2034088_2034097_2033887,00.html.

29. Civil libertarian Glenn Greenwald, for instance, has defended the Supreme Court's ruling in *Citizens United v. FEC* by conflating limits on campaign advertising with prohibiting organized groups of people from "expressing political views." Is a limit on duration of speech, location of speech, or the amount of money spent advertising that speech really equivalent to a prohibition of that viewpoint? See Greenwald's opinion in *Salon*, January 2, 2010, http://www.salon.com /2010/01/22/citizens_united/.

30. Senator Paul Simon quoted on *60 Minutes*, CBS, December 17, 1995.

31. Senator Bill Bradley in a speech at the John F. Kennedy School of Government, January 16, 1996.

32. Richard S. Wurman, *Information Anxiety* (New York: Doubleday, 1987), p. 32.

33. Americans consume twelve hours of information a day, outside work. This double-counts multitasking (watching TV while reading the newspaper and checking social media), but the researchers estimate three-quarters of our waking time at home is spent consuming information. See http://ijoc.org/index.php/ijoc/article/viewFile /1566/743.

34. This limit is known as Miller's law. See http://www.human-memory. net/types_short.html.

35. Simon P. Anderson and André de Palma, "Competition for Attention in the Information (Overload) Age," https://www.business.unsw.edu.au / About-Site/Schools-Site/Economics-Site/Documents/S.%20 Anderson%20-%20Competition%20for%20Attention%20in%20the%20 Information%20(Overload)%20Age.pdf.

36. Herbert A. Simon, as quoted by Sam Anderson, "In Defense of Distraction," *New York*, May 17, 2009, http://nymag.com/news/features/56793/.

37. See http://www.cjr.org/overload/interview_with_clay_shirky_par.php ?page=all.

38. See Senator Pat Roberts comments in *Congressional Record*, March 12, 1997, p. S2178: "This resolution—not the intent, but this resolution—in terms of practical effect is tyranny. Adopt it and wonder whether *Common Sense* could exist in our time in terms of

public distribution and dissemination and understanding. This resolution is tyranny of the worst kind: government tyranny. Adopt it and wonder whether *The Federalist Papers,* written by James Madison and John Jay to influence voters in New York to adopt a new Constitution could, in fact, exist in our time."

39. The first editions of *Common Sense* sold for either one or two shillings. See Megan Mulder's article "Common Sense by Thomas Paine" in the Z. Smith Reynolds Library of Wake Forest University, http://zsr.wfu.edu/special/blog/common-sense-by-thomas-paine-1776/, for details on the early printing contracts.

40. Non-subscribers to the newspapers that originally published *The Federalist* were able to purchase a bound edition of them for eight shillings according to Matthew Garrett, *Episodic Poetics: Politics and Literary Form After the Constitution* (New York: Oxford University Press, 2014), p. 167, n. 24.

41. Dan Sisson, *The American Revolution of 1800,* 40th anniversary ed. (San Francisco: Berrett-Koehler, 2014), p. 50.

42. Henry Augustine Washington, *The Writings of Thomas Jefferson* (Washington, DC: Taylor and Maury, 1853), p. 362.

43. Paul Leicester Ford, *The True George Washington* (Philadelphia: J. B. Lippincott Co., 1896), p. 297, and Center for Responsive Politics, "A Brief History of Money in Politics," 1995.

44. Zephyr Teachout, *Corruption in America* (Cambridge: Harvard University Press, 2014), p. 109.

45. Justice Stevens' concurrence to *Nixon v. Shrink Missouri Government PAC,* January 24, 2000, http://www.law.cornell.edu/supct/html/98-963 .ZC.html.

46. Transcript of oral arguments before the Supreme Court of the United States, March 24, 2009, p. 27, http://www.supremecourt.gov/oral _arguments/argument_transcripts/08-205.pdf. "Express advocacy" is a term used in the Bipartisan Campaign Reform Act to define speech that is considered electioneering.

47. ACLU letter opposing a constitutional amendment to overturn *Buckley v. Valeo,* as printed in *Congressional Record,* March 18, 1997, p. S2392.

48. *Congressional Record,* September 9, 2014, p. S5424, https://www .congress.gov/crec/2014/09/09/CREC-2014-09-09-senate.pdf.

49. Jonathan Soros, "Big Money Can't Buy Elections: Influence is Something Else," Reuters, February 10, 2015, http://blogs.reuters. com/great-debate/2015/02/09/soros-there-is-no-idyllic-pre-citizens -united-era-to-return-to/.

50. Paul Abowd, "Obscure Nonprofit Threatens Campaign Finance Limits beyond Montana," Center for Public Integrity, October 22,

2012, http://www.publicintegrity.org/2012/10/22/11577/obscure
-nonprofit-threatens-campaign-finance-limits-beyond-montana.

51. Mega-donor Sheldon Adelson, for example, has circumvented Israeli
campaign finance laws by purchasing and subsidizing free newspapers
that were in effect campaign advertisements. See Thomas Friedman,
"Is It Sheldon Adelson's World?" *New York Times,* March 11, 2015,
http://www.nytimes.com/2015/03/11/opinion/thomas-l-friedman-is-it
-sheldons-world.html?ref=topics

52. *Congressional Record,* March 12, 1997, p. S2174.

53. *Citizens United v. Gessler,* US Court of Appeals, Tenth Circuit,
November 12, 2014, https://www.ca10.uscourts.gov/opinions/14/14
-1387.pdf.

54. Quoted in Milton Gwirtzman's "The Supreme Problem," *Washington
Post,* January 12, 1997.

55. For more on this topic, see Jeff Clements, *Corporations Are Not People*
(San Francisco: Berrett-Koehler, 2014).

56. See http://www.scientificamerican.com/article/do-people-only-use
-10-percent-of-their-brains/.

57. See https://www.opensecrets.org/bigpicture/donordemographics.
php?cycle=2012. In the 2000 election cycle, 0.45 percent made a
contribution to a candidate, party, or political committee of $200 or
more. See "The Best Elections Money Can Buy," US PIRG, November
2000.

58. Chuck Todd explained in the lead-in: "You have to find out if you have
a sugar daddy or sugar mommy that can write you a check for a billion
dollars or knows people that can accumulate a billion dollars . . . I
think this whole process, it's the money. It's media, social media,
opposition research, the destructive nature of American discourse . . .
You have an accumulating effect that drives good people from running
for office." For the full quote on the collective intelligence of Congress,
see http://www.huffingtonpost.com/2014/11/20/chuck-todd-congress-iq-
dropping-larry-king-video_n_6193556.html?utm_hp_ref=tw.

59. Center for Responsive Politics, "Donor Demographics,"
https://www.opensecrets.org/overview/donordemographics.php.

60. Quoting Harri Oinas-Kukkonen, professor of information systems at
the University of Oulu, Finland, in *Knowledge Management:
Theoretical Foundation* (Informing Science Press, 2008), p. 181.

61. Ibid., p. 185.

62. Ibid.

63. *Congressional Record,* March 2, 1997.

64. See, for example, this 2001 ACLU statement opposing limits on
contributions to political parties, saying the organization supports
"expanding, not limiting" political speech: https://www.aclu.org/free
-speech/aclu-statement-campaign-finance-reform. See also the

ACLU's post-*Citizens United* statement wanting to "expand, not limit, the resources available to political advocacy" (https://www.aclu.org /free-speech/aclu-and-citizens-united) or ACLU testimony before the Senate Rules Committee on February 1, 1996, saying "the ACLU has long suggested that the way to solve the problems of campaign finance is to expand political participation for all legally qualified candidates, without conditions or limitations, not to restrict contributions and expenditures." Several former leaders of the ACLU disagree with the organization's position. For instance, see http://www.nationallawjournal .com/legaltimes/id=1202669239195/Former-ACLU-Leaders-Quarrel -With-Current-Leadership-Over-Campaign-Finance?slreturn =20150009173020.

65. Shane Goldmacher, "Websites Are Already Selling Out of Ad Inventory for 2016," *National Journal*, May 13, 2016, http://www.nationaljournal.com/2016-elections/websites-are -already-selling-out-of-ad-inventory-for-2016-20150512.

66. Fatimah Waseem, "Fewer US Adults Are Smoking," *USA Today*, June 18, 2013, http://www.usatoday.com/story/news/nation/2013/06/18 /smoking-rate-for-adults-declines-cdc-report-shows/2434525/.

67. Martha Gardner and Alan Brandt, "The Doctor's Choice Is America's Choice," *American Journal of Public Health*, February 2006, p. 222, http://www.ncbi.nlm.nih.gov/pmc/articles/PMC1470496/.

68. K. M. Cummings, C. P. Morley, and A. Hyland, "Failed Promises of the Cigarette Industry and Its Effect on Consumer Misperceptions about the Health Risks of Smoking," *Tobacco Control Journal*, 2002, vol. 11, p. 110, http://tobaccocontrol.bmj.com/content/11/suppl_1/i110.full.

69. Centers for Disease Control and Prevention, "Morbidity and Mortality Weekly Report," August 3, 2012, pp. 565–569, http://www.cdc.gov/mmwr/preview/mmwrhtml/mm6130a1.htm.

70. "Smoking Them Out," US PIRG, 1996.

71. Ibid.

72. Letter from Senators Orrin Hatch, Mitch McConnell, and Malcolm Wallop to DHHS, as reproduced in the National Cancer Institute's *Smoking and Tobacco Control Monograph 16*, chapter 8, "Tobacco Industry Challenge to ASSIST," by Jenny White and Lisa Bero: http://cancercontrol.cancer.gov/brp/tcrb/monographs/16/m16_8.pdf.

73. Fred Monardi and Stan Glanz, "Are Tobacco Industry Campaign Contributions Influencing State Legislative Behavior?" *American Journal of Public Health*, June 1998, vol. 88, no. 6, p. 918, http://www.ncbi.nlm.nih.gov/pmc/articles/PMC1508208/pdf /amjph00018-0060.pdf.

74. Devan Schwartz, "Most Northwest Residents Say They Want Labeling of Genetically Modified Food," *Oregon Public Broadcasting*, July 7,

2014, http://earthfix.opb.org/communities/article/most-northwest -residents-say-they-want-labeling-fo/.

75. Lee Drutman, "The Political One Percent of the One Percent," Sunlight Foundation, December 13, 2012, http://sunlightfoundation .com/blog/2011/12/13/the-political-one-percent-of-the-one-percent/.

76. Ibid.

77. Ken Vogel, "Big Money Breaks Out," *Politico*, December 29, 2014, http://www.politico.com/story/2014/12/top-political-donors-113833 .html.

78. Adam Lioz and Dana Mason, "Look Who's Not Coming to Washington," US Public Interest Research Group, 2005, http://www.policyarchive.org/handle/10207/6405.

79. Rachel Moskowitz, Fay Lomax Cook, and Benjamin Page, "Wealthy Americans, Philanthropy, and the Common Good," Russell Sage Foundation, September 25, 2011. http://www.scribd.com/doc/75022549 /Wealthy-Americans-Philanthropy-and-the-Common-Good

80. Adam Lioz, counsel at Demos, testimony before the US Senate, June 24, 2012, http://www.demos.org/publication/senate-testimony-adam -lioz-counsel-demos-taking-back-our-democracy-responding-citizens -u#_ftn7.

81. Robert McFadden, "Charles Keating, 90, Key Figure in '80s Savings and Loan Crisis, Dies," *New York Times*, April 2, 2014, http://www.nytimes.com/2014/04/02/business/charles-keating-key -figure-in-the-1980s-savings-and-loan-crisis-dies-at-90.html?_r=0.

82. Matt Schundel, "Charles H. Keating Jr., Central Figure in Savings-and-Loan Scandal, Dies at 90," *Washington Post*, April 2, 2014, http://www.washingtonpost.com/national/charles-h-keating-jr-central -figure-in-savings-and-loan-scandal-dies-at-90/2014/04/02/a53cf6f6 -ba81-11e3-9c3c-311301e2167d_story.html.

83. Ibid.

84. This according to a 1994 Yankelovic poll as cited in "10 Myths About Money in Politics," Center for Responsive Politics.

85. Martin Gilens, *Affluence and Influence* (Princeton, NJ: Princeton University Press, 2012), p. 4.

86. Lawrence R. Jacobs and Robert Y. Shapiro, "Politicians Don't Pander," *Washington Post*, March 19, 2000.

87. See http://www.merriam-webster.com/dictionary/corruption.

88. You may notice that the Supreme Court, and lawyers in general, strive to present the appearance of being smarter than ordinary citizens— whom they expect to submit to their superior intellects. So, they use inscrutable phrases like "quid pro quo" when they could use terms that most people would understand, such as "tit for tat" or "bribery." This is a common trick of the weakest branch of our government,

which has no real authority to make citizens obey it, so it relies on puffery and stature.

89. Adam Lioz, "Breaking the Vicious Cycle," *Seton Hall Law Review*, vol. 43, no. 4 (2013), p. 1269.

90. "Coming to Terms," Center for Responsive Politics, 1995.

91. Bill Moyers, *Moyers on Democracy* (New York: Anchor Books, 2009), p. 187.

92. In fact, Anthony Kennedy, Antonin Scalia, and Clarence Thomas have all written that courts should void limits on direct contributions to candidates, so they do not believe that even direct contributions are corrupting.

93. Gerald Fraser, "Last Senate Race Debate Marked by Harsh Charges," *New York Times*, November 2, 1970. Buckley and his two opponents "all agreed campaign spending should be limited."

94. Roger Sherman, "A Brief Review of the Legislation Against Corrupt Practices at Elections," Hamilton Club of Chicago, 1898, p. 74.

95. Marc Yacker, "Major Events in the History of Federal Campaign Reform in the United States," Congressional Research Service, Library of Congress, March 7, 1974, p. 1.

96. It is noteworthy that even in dissenting to the 1941 *United States v. Classic* opinion, Justice William O. Douglas was concerned about money influencing election outcomes, not influencing legislators themselves. He wrote that "the Constitution should be read as to give Congress an expansive implied power to place beyond the pale acts which, in their direct or indirect effect, impair the integrity of Congressional elections. For when corruption enters, the election is no longer free, the choice of the people is affected." See Teachout, *Corruption in America*, p. 192.

97. See bonus chapter 9 of this book for more details: www.WhenMoneyTalks.com.

98. *Buckley v. Valeo*, US Court of Appeals, District of Columbia Circuit, August 15, 1975, http://openjurist.org/519/f2d/821.

99. Ibid.

100. Ibid.

101. See http://billmoyers.com/content/the-powell-memo-a-call-to-arms-for-corporations/ for details on the Powell memo.

102. David Firestone, "Adhering to a Justices Spirit, Not Footsteps," *New York Times*, May 12, 1998, quotes Joshua Rosenkranz, a clerk of Brennan's, saying that Justice Brennan agreed to lend his name to the Brennan Center for Justice on the condition that the center "never pledge allegiance to any particular opinion of his, but rather that we be moved by the spirit of the Brennan legacy."

103. *Buckley v. Valeo,* US Supreme Court, 1976.

104. Skelly Wright, "Politics and the Constitution: Is Money Speech?" *Yale Law Journal,* vol. 85, no. 8, 1976.

105. Joshua Rosenkranz, *Buckley Stops Here* (New York: Century Foundation Press, 1998), p. 27.

106. *Buckley v. Valeo,* 1976.

107. US Supreme Court, *First National Bank of Boston v. Bellotti,* 1978.

108. *National Black Police v. District of Columbia Board of Elections,* District of Columbia District Court, April 18, 1996, http://www.plainsite.org/dockets/220zqa7kv/district-of-columbia -district-court/nat-black-police-v-dist-of-col-bd-of-elections/.

109. Judge Melvin Brunetti, dissenting to *Vannatta v. Keisling,* US Court of Appeals, Ninth Circuit, 1998.

110. *Alaska v. Alaska ACLU,* Supreme Court of Alaska, April 16, 1999.

111. Jeanne Bassett, "Freedom to Spend Is Not Freedom of Speech," *Albuquerque Tribune,* September 18, 1998.

112. Center for Responsive Politics report quoted in the ruling *Kruse v. Cincinnati,* US Court of Appeals, Sixth Circuit, 1998.

113. Judge Cornelia Kennedy in the majority opinion of *Kruse v. Cincinnati.*

114. Judge Jack Sandstorm, *Montana Right to Life v. Eddleman,* US Court of Appeals, Ninth Circuit, September 19, 2000.

115. Judge William Sessions, *Landell v. Sorrell,* US District Court of Vermont, August 10, 2000.

116. Justice David Souter, *Nixon v. Shrink Missouri Government PAC,* US Supreme Court, 2000.

117. *Austin v. Michigan Chamber of Commerce,* US Supreme Court, 1990.

118. Eric Boehlert, "You Can't Teach an Old Attack Dog New Tricks," *Salon,* July 20, 2004, http://www.salon.com/2004/07/20/david _bossie/.

119. Jeffrey Toobin, "Money Unlimited" *New Yorker,* May 21, 2012, http://www.newyorker.com/magazine/2012/05/21/money -unlimited.

120. Ibid.

121. *Citizens United v. FEC,* US Supreme Court, 2010.

122. Justice Byron White, dissent to *Buckley v. Valeo,* US Supreme Court, 1976.

123. See Thom Hartmann, *Unequal Protection* (San Francisco: Berrett-Koehler, 2010) for details.

124. *Arizona Free Enterprise v. Bennett,* US Supreme Court, 2011.

125. *McCutcheon v. FEC,* US Supreme Court, 2014.

126. *Williams-Yulee v. Florida,* US Supreme Court, 2015.

127. Larry Kramer, *The People Themselves: Popular Constitutionalism and Judicial Review* (New York: Oxford University Press, 2004), especially chapter 3.

128. Ibid., p. 114.

129. James MacGregor Burns, *Packing the Court* (New York: Penguin Press, 2009), p. 73.

130. Mark Tushnet, *Taking the Constitution Away from the Courts* (Princeton, NJ: Princeton University Press, 1999).

131. "Supreme Court Decisions Overruled by Subsequent Decision," appendix to Senate Document No. 103-6, 103rd Congress, Government Printing Office, 1996.

132. Pam Karlan, for instance, has been critical of limits on big money in politics (see Samuel Issacharoff and Pamel S. Karlan, "The Hydraulics of Campaign Finance Reform," *Texas Law Review*, vol. 77, no. 7, June 1999) but is considered a potential nominee by President Obama. See http://thinkprogress.org/justice/2013/05/23/2044771/ten-potential-democratic-supreme-court-nominees-who-arent-named-sri-srinivasan/.

133. Kathleen Sullivan, for instance, has said all constitutional amendments pose a danger of "mutiny against the authority of the Supreme Court." See *Great and Extraordinary Occasions: Developing Guidelines for Constitutional Change* (New York: Century Foundation Press, 1999), p. 42.

134. Tushnet, *Taking the Constitution Away from the Courts*, p. 180, emphasis original.

135. Similarly, our Fourteenth Amendment did not go through the traditional ratification process by winning approval of three-fourths of elected state legislatures. Nonetheless, we accepted it. The election of 1868 in essence allowed the people of the nation to speak on the question of Reconstruction, and they ratified it by sending a strong Republican majority to Congress to implement it.

136. Bruce Ackerman, *We The People: Foundations* (Cambridge: Belknap Press of Harvard University Press, 1991).

137. Bruce Ackerman, *We the People: Transformations* (Cambridge: Belknap Press of Harvard University Press, 1998), p. 262.

138. Ralph Goldman, "The Advisory Referendum in America," *Public Opinion Quarterly*, Summer 1950, p. 310.

139. Ackerman, *We the People: Transformations*, p. 297.

140. Ibid., p. 316.

141. Robert Peterson, "Supreme Court: Impeach 'Oligarchy' Now in Power," *Missoulian*, July 13, 2014, http://missoulian.com/news/opinion/mailbag/supreme-court-impeach-oligarchy-now-in-power/article_76cd196a-0921-11e4-8217-001a4bcf887a.html.

142. David Savage, "Newt Gingrich Says He'd Defy Supreme Court Rulings He Opposed," *Los Angeles Times*, December 17, 2011.

143. Rob Hager and James Marc Leas, "Why a Constitutional Amendment Isn't Needed to Overturn 'Citizens United'," Counterpunch.org, July 9, 2012, http://www.counterpunch.org/2012/07/09/why-a-constitutional-amendment-isnt-needed-to-overturn-citizens-united/.

144. Ibid.

145. Thomas Jefferson, "Draft of the Kentucky Resolutions," *The Political Writings of Thomas Jefferson* (Thomas Jefferson Memorial Foundation, 1993), p. 127.

146. Akhil Reed Amar, *The Bill of Rights* (New Haven, CT: Yale University Press, 1998), p. 40.

147. Ibid., p. 41.

148. Tenth Amendment Center, "Glover, Booth, and Paine: Over 150 Years of Nullification," http://tenthamendmentcenter.com/2014/04/13/glover-booth-and-paine-over-150-years-of-nullification/.

149. Senate Joint Resolution 2, 105th Congress, first session, introduced January 21, 1997.

150. *Congressional Record*, March 18, 1997, p. S2389.

151. Ibid.

152. *Congressional Record*, March 18, 1997 p. S2390.

153. *Congressional Record*, March 12, 1997, p. S2179.

154. *Congressional Record*, March 12, 1997, p. S2193.

155. Jonathan Bingham, "Democracy of Plutocracy: The Case for a Constitutional Amendment to Overturn *Buckley v. Valeo*," *Annals of the American Academy*, July 1986, as printed in the *Congressional Record*, February 14, 1995, p. S2631.

156. *Congressional Record*, March 12, 1997, p. S2176. Senator Hollings elaborates: "I know the mechanics of political campaigns, and when you have an opponent with $100,000 and I have $1 million, all I need do is just lay low. He only has $100,000 and I know that he wants to wait until October when the people finally turn their interest to the general election. . . . And then I let go, come October 10. That is three to four weeks leading into the campaign, and I have yard signs, radio for the farmer in the early morning. I have early morning driving-to-work radio, I have radio for the college students. I know how to tailor make with my million bucks, and I can tell you by November 1, after three weeks of that, my opponent's family has said 'What is the matter? Why are you not answering? Are you not interested anymore?' I have, through wealth, taken away his speech."

157. House Joint Resolution 47, introduced in the first session of the 105th Congress, February 10, 1997.

158. Press release by Senator Robert C. Byrd, March 18, 1997.

159. House Joint Resolution 20, introduced in the first session of the 113th Congress on January 22, 2013.

160. Senate Joint Resolution 19, 113th Congress, second session, as amended, July 17, 2014.

161. John Paul Stevens, *Six Amendments: How and Why We Should Change the Constitution* (New York: Little, Brown and Company, 2014), p. 79.

162. David Gans and Ryan Woo, "Reversing *Citizens United*: Lessons from the Sixteenth Amendment," Constitutional Accountability Center, January 12, 2012, p. 7, http://theusconstitution.org/sites/default/files/briefs/Download%20Reversing%20Citizens%20United%20Here.pdf.

163. See Bruce Ackerman, *We the People: Foundations*.

164. Jay Bybee, "Ulysses at the Mast: Democracy, Federalism, and the Sirens' Song of the Seventeenth Amendment," *Scholarly Works*, Paper 350, p. 536, http://scholars.law.unlv.edu/cgi/viewcontent.cgi?article=1365&context=facpub.

165. "Decline of the Senate," *Wall Street Journal*, August 24, 1905, p. 1, as cited in Joseph Friedman, "The Rapid Sequence of Events Forcing the Senate's Hand: A Reappraisal of the Seventeenth Amendment," *CUREJ: College Undergraduate Research Electronic Journal*, University of Pennsylvania, March 30, 2009, p. 8, http://repository.upenn.edu/curej/93.

166. "Election of Senators," *Los Angeles Times*, July 5, 1905, as cited in Joseph Friedman, "The Rapid Sequence of Events Forcing the Senate's Hand," p. 8, http://repository.upenn.edu/curej/93.

167. Ibid.

168. Ibid., p. 39.

169. Robert Luce, *Legislative Principles: The History and Theory of Lawmaking by Representative Government*, 1930, p. 449.

170. These paragraphs are borrowed from Derek Cressman's "Ties that Bind," Common Cause white paper, September 2012.

171. John Dickinson, *The Letters of Fabius*, 1788, letter 8, p. 70, http://deila.dickinson.edu/cdm/compoundobject/collection/ownwords/id/274.

172. Kris Kobach, "May 'We The People' Speak? The Forgotten Role of Constituent Instructions in Amending the Constitution," *UC Davis Law Review*, vol. 33, no. 1, 1999, p. 76.

173. Ralph Goldman "The Advisory Referendum in America," *Public Opinion Quarterly*, Summer 1950, p. 308.

174. It is particularly significant that the New York legislature obeyed its instructions on prison labor because in the same election voters replaced Democrats in control of the legislature with a Republican majority and the Republican Party opposed abolishing prison labor.

175. Arkansas, Illinois, Indiana, Maine, Massachusetts, Michigan, New Hampshire, North Carolina, Ohio, Tennessee, and Vermont all had the right to instruct as part of their state constitutions at one time.

176. Article I, Section 10 of the California 1849 constitution. This provision has been maintained in subsequent versions and is now found in Article I, Section 3(a).

177. The delegate said, "It is high time to discard the phraseology which belongs to the old system of petitioning a superior power. The same power that enables the people to govern themselves, surely gives them a right to remedy their grievances." Quoted in Steve Mayer and Ronald Fein, amicus brief by Free Speech For People to the California Supreme Court, *Howard Jarvis Taxpayers Association v. Debra Bowen*, no. S220289, Supreme Court of California, p. 2.

178. Ibid., p. 3.

179. Ibid., p. 4.

180. Friedman, "The Rapid Sequence of Events Forcing the Senate's Hand," p. 53, http://repository.upenn.edu/curej/93.

181. David Schleicher, "The Seventeenth Amendment and Federalism in an Age of National Political Parties," George Mason University Law and Economic Research Paper Series, no. 13-33, p. 15, http://papers.ssrn.com/sol3/papers.cfm?abstract_id=2269077.

182. Bybee, "Ulysses at the Mast," p. 538.

183. Friedman, "The Rapid Sequence of Events Forcing the Senate's Hand," p. 71.

184. Skelly Wright, "Politics and the Constitution: Is Money Speech?" *Yale Law Journal*, vol. 85, no. 8, 1979, p. 1005.

185. *Congressional Record*, Ninety-Seventh Congress, 128 (81), p. H3901.

186. Cosponsors included Representatives Millicent Fenwick (R-NJ), Barbara Mikulski (D-MD), Tom Bevill (D-AL), Brian Donnelly (D-MA), Norman D'Amours (D-NH), Robert Edgar (D-PA), John LaFalce (D-NY), and Howard Wolpe (D-MI).

187. Lloyd Cutler as cited by Senator Ernest Hollings, *Congressional Record*, March 13, 1997, p. S2244.

188. Senate roll call, April 22, 1988.

189. Senate roll call, May 27, 1993.

190. Senate roll call, February 14, 1995.

191. Quoted by Gene Karpinski, executive director of US PIRG, in testimony on campaign finance reform before the House

Subcommittee on the Constitution of the House Judiciary
Committee, February 27, 1997.

192. Poll by Mario Brossard for the *Washington Post,* January 14–19, 1997.

193. *Congressional Record,* January 21, 1997, p. S556.

194. Charles Pope, "Senate Soundly Rejects a Measure to Limit Spending on Campaigns," *Philadelphia Inquirer,* March 19, 1997.

195. "Cheaper Campaigns Won't Wound Our Freedoms," *Buffalo News,* March 22, 1997.

196. "Dear colleague" letter from Russ Feingold and Edward Kennedy, January 23, 1997.

197. Most of the campaign reform community was focused on incremental measures, such as reinstating contribution limits for political parties, and saw the amendment vote as a distraction. Senator Mitch McConnell gloated at the opposition from reformers to the Hollings amendment, saying "Even Common Cause is against this proposal. Even the *Washington Post* is against this proposal. Even Senator McCain and Senator Feingold, I believe, are going to oppose this."

198. Transcript from "Removing Obstacles to Campaign Finance Reform: Why Not a Constitutional Amendment?" Harvard Law School Electoral Reform Project, April 2000.

199. "Free Speech For People Nationwide Voter Survey," Hart Research Associates, December 2010–January 2011, http://freespeechforpeople.org/sites/default/files/FSFP%20Nationwide%20Voter%20Survey-1.pdf.

200. "Super PACs Having Negative Impact, Say Voters Aware of 'Citizens United' Ruling," Pew Research Center for the People & the Press, http://www.people-press.org/files/legacy-pd/1-17-12%20Campaign%20Finance.pdf.

201. Derek Cressman, "Time to Amend: No More Half Measures in Campaign Finance Reform," *Washington Monthly,* December 29, 2011, http://www.washingtonmonthly.com/ten-miles-square/2011/12/time_to_amend034394.php?page=all&print=true.

202. See http://sos.mt.gov/elections/2012/BallotIssues/I-166.pdf for the official ballot language.

203. Amendment 65 on the Colorado ballot, November 2012. See https://www.colorado.gov/pacific/sites/default/files/2012%20English%20Blue%20Book%20Internet%20Version.pdf.

204. See http://democracyamendmentmass.org/files/2012/10/Ballot-Question-District-and-Town-List-with-Question-Numbers1.pdf.

205. Paul Blumenthal, "Citizens United Rejected by Voters in Montana, Colorado," *Huffington Post,* November 7, 2012, http://www.huffingtonpost.com/2012/11/07/citizens-united-rejected-montana-colorado_n_2089949.html.

206. Jess Bravin "Montana Voters' Verdict: Supreme Court Was Wrong," *Wall Street Journal Law Blog,* November 8, 2012, http://blogs.wsj.com /law/2012/11/08/montana-voters-verdict-supreme-court-was-wrong/.

207. "Montanans Take a Stand" *New York Times,* November 16, 2012, http://www.nytimes.com/2012/11/17/opinion/montanans-take-a-stand .html?partner=rssnyt&emc=rss&_r=4&.

208. *Cook v. Gralike,* US Supreme Court, 2001.

209. "Fighting Ballot Bloat in California: The Prop 49 Ruling," *Los Angeles Times,* August 12, 2014.

210. Goodwin Liu, concurring in *Howard Jarvis Taxpayers Association v. Bowen,* Grant of Writ of Mandamus, August 11, 2014.

211. See http://www.huffingtonpost.com/campus-election-engagement -project/mark-udall-vs-cory-gardne_b_6000876.html.

212. Harvard academic Larry Lessig, for instance, waged a $10 million campaign targeting ten races and trying to elevate the notion of corruption without tying it to any specific solution.

213. McConnell's letter was reported in the *Washington Post,* November 27, 1995.

214. Larry Lessig, *Republic Lost: How Money Corrupts Congress—and a Plan to Stop It* (New York; Twelve/Hachette Book Group, 2011), p. 97.

215. See W. W. Willoughby quoted in Ralph Goldman, "The Advisory Referendum in America," *Public Opinion Quarterly,* vol. 14, no. 2, Summer 1950, p. 311.

216. Ibid., p. 312.

217. Ibid.

218. See www.NationalPopularVote.com.

219. *Congressional Record,* March 13, 1997.

220. John Gardner, *No Easy Victories* (Harper & Row, New York, 1968), p. 84.

Recommended Reading

Ackerman, Bruce. *We the People: Foundations*. Cambridge: Harvard University Press, 1991.

Ackerman, Bruce. *We the People: Transformations*. Cambridge: Harvard University Press, 1998.

Amar, Akhil Reed. *The Bill of Rights*. New Haven, CT: Yale University Press, 1998.

Amar, Akhil Reed, and Alan Hirsch. *For the People*. New York: The Free Press, 1998.

Brookings Institution. *Campaign Finance Reform: A Sourcebook*. Washington, DC: Brookings Institution Press, 1997.

Burns, James MacGregor. *Packing the Court*. New York: Penguin Press, 2009.

Century Foundation. *Great and Extraordinary Occasions: Developing Guidelines for Constitutional Change*. New York: Century Foundation Press, 1999.

Clements, Jeffrey D. *Corporations Are Not People*, 2nd ed., San Francisco: Berrett-Koehler, 2014.

Drew, Elizabeth. *The Corruption of American Politics*. Secaucus, NJ: Birch Lane Press, 1999.

Haddock, Doris, with Dennis Burke. *Granny D: A Memoir*. New York: Villard, 2003.

Hartmann, Thom. *Unequal Protection: How Corporations Became "People"—and How You Can Fight Back*. San Francisco: Berrett-Koehler, 2010.

Harvard Law School Electoral Reform Project. *Removing Obstacles to Campaign Finance Reform: Why Not a Constitutional Amendment*. Transcript of April 2000 workshop.

Kramer, Larry D. *The People Themselves*. New York: Oxford University Press, 2004.

Lasch, Christopher. *The Revolt of the Elites and the Betrayal of Democracy*. New York: W. W. Norton & Company, 1995.

Lessig, Lawrence. *Republic Lost: How Money Corrupts Congress—and a Plan to Stop It*. New York: Twelve/Hachette Book Group, 2011.

Nichols, John, and Robert W. McChesney. *Dollaracracy: How the Money and Media Election Complex Is Destroying America*. New York: Nation Books, 2013.

Paine, Thomas. *Common Sense: 200th Anniversary Edition*. New York: Penguin Group, 2003.

Parker, Richard D. *Here the People Rule*. Cambridge: Harvard University Press, 1994.

Peterson, Merrill D. *The Political Writings of Thomas Jefferson*. Woodlawn: Thomas Jefferson Memorial Foundation, 1993

Phillips, Kevin. *Wealth and Democracy*. New York: Broadway Books, 2002.

Post, Robert C. *Citizens Divided*. Cambridge: Harvard University Press, 2014.

Raskin, Jamin B., and John Bonifaz. *The Wealth Primary*. Washington, DC: Center for Responsive Politics, 1994.

Rosenkranz, Joshua. *Buckley Stops Here*. New York: Century Foundation Press, 1998.

Sisson, Dan, and Thom Hartmann. *The American Revolution of 1800*. San Francisco: Berrett-Koehler, 2014.

Stevens, John Paul. *Six Amendments*. New York: Little, Brown and Company, 2014.

Teachout, Zephyr. *Corruption in America*. Cambridge: Harvard University Press, 2014.

Tushnet, Mark. *Taking the Constitution Away from the Courts*. Princeton, NJ: Princeton University Press, 1999.

Acknowledgments

Most of the ideas, strategies, and tactics in this book are not mine. I am indebted to countless Americans who came before me, innovating their way toward self-government. My contribution, hopefully, is to apply these ideas to our current crisis of money in politics. There are some Americans in particular I should thank for advancing the idea that "We the People" should overturn our Supreme Court and its misguided ruling that money is speech.

This book is dedicated to Senator Ernest "Fritz" Hollings, who was first elected on a campaign budget of $100 and who became the leading champion of a constitutional amendment to limit big money in politics during his time in the US Senate. For years, Senator Hollings quite literally carried an amendment in his suit pocket, ready to lay it on the desk of the Senate when a procedural opportunity arose. Thanks also go to his loyal staffer, Joey Lesesne.

This book is in memory of Larry Hansen, Harry Lonsdale, and Bob Edgar—none of whom lived to see *Buckley* reversed but each of whom inspired many of us to keep trying.

Thanks to fellow travelers John Bonifaz, Jon Goldin-Dubois, Karen Hobert Flynn, Adam Lioz, Pete Maysmith, Kai Newkirk, and Brenda Wright. May this book push you forward as much as you have lifted me.

Voters in Montana, Colorado, Massachusetts, and California and in San Francisco, Los Angeles, and Chicago would not have had the chance to instruct Congress on this issue without the work and perseverance of C. B. Pearson,

Matt Leow, and Jon Motl of Stand with Montanans; Elena Nunez and Arn Pearson of Common Cause; Faye Park of the Public Interest Network; Annie Sanders of Colorado Fair Share; San Francisco supervisor John Avalos; California senator Ted Lieu; California assembly member Bob Wieckowski; Los Angeles city councilor Richard Alarcon; California Common Cause organizer Anjuli Kronheim; Richmond city councilor Jim Rogers; Pam Wilmot and Tyler Creighton of Massachusetts Common Cause; Rey Lopez Calderon, Brian Gladstein, and Benjamin Singer of Common Cause Illinois; and Michele Sutter and the whole gang at the Money Out Voters In coalition. Special thanks to Fred Woocher, Ron Rein, Steve Meyer, and Tom Donnelly for their efforts to get California's Proposition 49 back on the ballot.

Americans owe a debt to David Cobb, Caitlin Sopaci-Belknap, Kaja Rebane, and hundreds more for their truly tireless work at Move to Amend, as well as Donna Edwards and Craig McDonald for their pioneering work at the Center for a New Democracy (and subsequent bigger and better things).

Thanks to the many people whose support or adversity steeled my resolve to push this issue forward and helped sharpen the issue (some of whom may not agree with everything in this book), including Margie Alt, Susan Anderson, Marge Baker, Matt Baker, Craig Barnes, Emmet Bondurant, James Bopp, Kathay Feng, Gene Karpinski, Lisa Graves, Michael Keegan, Michael Keischnick, Art Lipson, Susan Lerner, Tom Lopach, Mitch McConnell, Burt Neuborne, Nick Nyhart, Miles Rapoport, Jamie Raskin, Robert Reich, Will Robinson, Josh Rosenkranz, Steve Silberstein, Stephen Spaulding, Bob Stern, Mary and Sarah Stranahan, Phillip

Ung, Alan and Jan Weirsba, Rob Weissman, Wendy Wendlandt, and Tracy Western.

Although this is not an academic book, the ideas in it have been influenced by several scholars who have documented and explained American traditions of self-governance, including Bruce Ackerman, Akhil Reed Amar, Larry Kramer, Richard Parker, and Mark Tushnet. Special thanks to James MacGregor Burns, who taught both the skills of book writing and fundamental aspects of American democracy and leadership at Williams College.

This book would never have happened without the support and encouragement of Jeff Clements, my wife Deniz, and Neal Maillet of Berrett-Koehler. And finally, this book would have been less clear without the masterful work of Jon S. Ford and Jonathan Peck to hone and polish the manuscript. Thank you.

About the Author

•Derek Cressman began working professionally to reduce big money in politics in 1995 with such nonpartisan organizations as Common Cause and the Public Interest Research Group. As US PIRG's democracy program director, he was the first professional advocate in Washington, DC, to support a constitutional amendment to limit campaign spending.

As director of Common Cause's Amend 2012 campaign, Derek was the architect behind voter instruction measures in Montana, Colorado, Massachusetts, and California, where voters demanded Congress pass an amendment to overturn the Supreme Court's ruling in *Citizens United v. FEC*.

In 2014, Derek Cressman ran for California secretary of state. Though he didn't win his election, the legislature responded to his campaign, and the efforts of others, by referring a question to the November 2014 ballot instructing Congress to overturn the *Citizens United* ruling—the central plank of Derek's campaign platform. Both during and after his campaign, Derek joined the March for Democracy from Los Angeles to Sacramento, culminating in a nonviolent civil disobedience where many activists were arrested for staging a sit-in at the state capitol.

Derek has testified before committees of the United States Senate, California State Assembly and Senate, and California Fair Political Practices Commission; served as an expert in federal litigation; and authored and coauthored numerous reports as well as one previous book, *The Recall's Broken Promise: How Big Money Still Runs California Politics*. Derek has appeared extensively in the media, including the Associated Press, *Roll Call*, *The Hill*, *National Journal*, *USA Today*, the *New York Times*, *Los Angeles Times*, *Christian Science Monitor*, *Washington Times*, *Boston Globe*, *San Francisco Chronicle*, *San Jose Mercury News*, *Sacramento Bee*, *Atlanta Journal-Constitution*, *Austin American-Statesman*, *Orlando Sentinel*, *Albuquerque Journal*, and *Kansas City Star*.

When he's not working to improve our democracy, Derek enjoys spending time with his wife and two daughters. He credits his time running marathons and mountaineering with building his fortitude to tackle obstacles like the US Supreme Court. He is an avid woodworker and picks at the banjo when he needs a break. Derek grew up in Colorado Springs and graduated cum laude from Williams College in 1990 with a degree in political science.

Connect with Derek

On Twitter @DerekCressman

www.facebook.com/CressmanConversations

E-Mail: derek@derekcressman.com

Websites: www.derekcressman.com and
www.whenmoneytalks.com

We Can Do It—How We Really Can Get Big Money Out of Politics

Thanks for reading *When Money Talks*! I know you agree that getting big money out of politics is vital to save our democracy. But even after reading this book and learning about how Americans have overturned misguided Supreme Court rulings in the past, you may be wondering if it's really possible to overturn *Citizens United* and establish that unlimited campaign spending isn't free speech. Cynics will tell you it can't be done while opponents will warn that free speech would grind to a halt if it happened. I've created an additional e-book with three bonus chapters to address these issues. You can download these chapters for free at:

www.whenmoneytalks.com.

Here's what you'll find:

Bonus Chapter A
We've Done it Before—How Legislators and Voters have Limited Money in Politics

This chapter reveals that, despite what you might think, Americans have been remarkably successful over our history in forcing Congress and the states to enact some very tough rules against big money in politics. The problem has been that these laws have not been enforced, in large part due to the courts.

Bonus Chapter B
Myths and Red Herrings—Faulty Arguments of the Big Money Believers

This chapter examines the supposed virtues that supporters of big money claim huge campaign spending has for democracy and details why they are wrong. It's a handy reference guide to prep for that conversation you'll have over Thanksgiving dinner or at a Starbucks with those rare folks who actually defend the *Citizens United* ruling.

Bonus Chapter C
The Real Threats to Free Speech—How Government Stifles Regular People While Letting Billionaires Shout

Money is not free speech and the Roberts Court is wrong to pretend otherwise. The debate over money in politics risks overshadowing what we mean by "free" speech in the first place. This chapter explores the challenges that ordinary people face in speaking their mind and the lack of support the courts are giving us.

Index

Berrett–Koehler
Publishers

Connecting people and ideas
to create a world that works for all

Dear Reader,

Thank you for picking up this book and joining our worldwide community of Berrett-Koehler readers. We share ideas that bring positive change into people's lives, organizations, and society.

To welcome you, we'd like to offer you a free e-book. You can pick from among twelve of our bestselling books by entering the promotional code **BKP92E** here: http://www.bkconnection.com/welcome.

When you claim your free e-book, we'll also send you a copy of our e-newsletter, the *BK Communiqué*. Although you're free to unsubscribe, there are many benefits to sticking around. In every issue of our newsletter you'll find

- A free e-book
- Tips from famous authors
- Discounts on spotlight titles
- Hilarious insider publishing news
- A chance to win a prize for answering a riddle

Best of all, our readers tell us, "Your newsletter is the only one I actually read." So claim your gift today, and please stay in touch!

Sincerely,

Charlotte Ashlock
Steward of the BK Website

Questions? Comments? Contact me at bkcommunity@bkpub.com.

Certified

Corporation
bcorporation.net